First published in 2017 by Barrallier Books Pty Ltd,
trading as Echo Books

Registered Offi ce: 35-37 Gordon Avenue, West Geelong, Victoria 3220, Australia.

www.echobooks.com.au

Copyright ©Marcus Fielding

National Library of Australia Cataloguing-in-Publication entry.

Creator: Fielding, Marcus, producer.

Title: In the field and on the field : a highlight history of the

Australian Army Rugby Union/Produced by Marcus Fielding.

ISBN: 9780648074540 (hardback)

Subjects: Rugby Union football players--Australia--Anecdotes. Rugby Union football--Australia--Anecdotes.
Rugby Union football--Tournaments--History.

Book layout and design by Peter Gamble, Canberra.
Set in Garamond Premier Pro Display, 12/17 and Optima Regular/Bold.

www.echobooks.com.au

www.armyrugby.org.au

IN THE FIELD & ON THE FIELD

A Highlight History of the Australian Army Rugby Union

produced by
Marcus Fielding

ECHO BOOKS

Contents

Foreword

Major General John Caligari,
DSC, AM

President of the Australian
Army Rugby Union

Rugby Union is a sporting code that has been played by generations of service people since the earliest days of Australia's armed forces.

The story of Rugby Union in the Australian Army is an important component of the Services rugby tradition, and indeed an integral part of the history of the code itself in Australia.

The Australian Army Rugby Union's (AARU) mission is to promote and develop Rugby Union throughout the Australian Army. In striving to fulfil that mission, the AARU commissioned a research project to produce a 'highlight' history of Rugby Union in the Australian Army.

The goals of the project were to:

- Recover, reconstruct and document as much of the AARU's history as possible.
- Strengthen the understanding of the AARU's place within the Army.
- Recognise key events, characters, stories and anecdotes about the AARU.

The history highlights the players, teams and events that have contributed to the development and successes of Army Rugby Union. It includes many of the key matches, results and anecdotes about the sport as it was played in Australia and abroad.

The AARU's ethos is based on the Army's values—courage, initiative and teamwork—and the history clearly demonstrates that it has and continues to be a central feature of the sport in the Australian Army. Indeed, the Army's values have been shaped by competition in sports like Rugby Union over a century.

Significantly, the project identified that the first truly representative Australian Army Rugby Union team was formed in 1919 in France immediately following the Armistice.

I am pleased to present this highlight history of the Rugby Union in the Australian Army.

Leather cover of a Rugby Union football used by Australian troops in matches played before the battle of Gaza in 1917.

The ball was retained by 2742 Sergeant Basil Lanser, who is said to have served with both 1st Australian Light Horse Regiment and the Australian Provost Corps in the Middle East. Lanser, who was born in the United Kingdom, spent some years in Australia before and after World War I, but eventually returned to the UK, where he died in the 1930s.

AWM REL/00651

Warm-up– The Early Years 1868-1918

Australian military involvement in the sport of Rugby Union can be traced back to the early part of the nineteenth century and the recording, by the Sydney Monitor, that private soldiers in the barracks 'are in the habit of amusing themselves with the game of football'. While the game was imported with early settlers and soldiers of the imperial regiments posted to the colonies of Australia, there was of course no 'Army' then as we know it today in the Australian colonies.

From the mid-1850s some very small units of Volunteers were formed in New South Wales (NSW) and Victoria. The imperial regiments were formally withdrawn in 1870. The Volunteer units gradually grew in number through most of the colonies but by the mid-1880s began to be replaced in part—but not entirely—by partially paid Militia forces. There were also a very small colonial cadre of permanent artillerymen and engineers in the coastal defences around the major cities.

In the decades that followed, the English game of Rugby Union emerged in NSW as a pre-eminent football code and an integral

A Rugby Union Match in Queensland in the early 1900s.
Private Collection

part of sporting activities amongst members of the Australian colonial military forces. In July 1868, for example, the 50th Queens Own Regiment won their match against the Sydney Football Club at Victoria Barracks and later in the year the University of Sydney won a match against the Royal Navy's HMS *Rosario*. Over the years, the first Rugby Union club established in Sydney, the Wallaroos, played numerous matches against local Militia teams, for example in 1871 against No. 10 Battery of the Volunteer Artillery.

Even after Federation in 1901, it took several years to establish a proper functioning and largely Militia based

Australian Army of which the permanent forces were a very small proportion. The new Australian Commonwealth government, being mostly short of money, spent as little as possible on defence in its first few years. Any organised sport among the new units of the Australian Army was therefore by its very nature *ad hoc,* no matter what in which State it was being played.

In the wake of a formal inspection visit to Australia by Lord Kitchener in 1910, a range of defence measures were undertaken by the Australian Government to improve Australian defences. Among the most important in terms of its bearing on the growth of Rugby Union in the Army was the establishment of the Royal Military College (RMC) at Duntroon. Rugby Union emerged as Duntroon's principal football code soon after the establishment of the College in 1911. Although there had been heated discussions about the code of football that would be played by College cadets, the decision in favour of Rugby Union was strongly influenced by the game's pre-eminent position in NSW and therefore Canberra as much as by the small numbers of cadets available from which teams were to be drawn. Simply put, the College could not carry teams from two competing codes and rugby won out.

Duntroon's first Rugby Union club was established by V. J. R. Miles, the professor of English, and on 15 July 1911 the First XV played its inaugural match against the local Queanbeyan team, the Warrigals (losing 12-nil). That year there were two more matches played against visiting sides and a total of seven matches in 1912. By 1913, a total of twelve matches had been scheduled. Duntroon won against Sydney's Great Public Schools on 9 June 1913 (12-nil) and played another five matches before an outbreak of smallpox in Sydney resulted in the cancellation of further matches. Further interruptions to the Rugby Union program occurred in 1914, again due to an outbreak of infectious disease—in this case, diphtheria.

The progress of Rugby Union during Duntroon's early years was, however, significantly influenced by other events beyond its control—most particularly the outbreak of the First World War (WWI) in August 1914 which resulted in a rapid depletion of players at the College as they were deployed to active service. The departure of the First Class cadets saw the loss of half the rugby team and by the end of the year all but two had gone to the War.

Yet, despite depleted numbers, Rugby Union continued to be played against visiting teams from Sydney Grammar, Newington College, The King's School, Sydney University, and, from 1916 a new competition against the Royal Australian Naval College (RANC) at Jervis Bay. The first match was played at Jervis Bay in September 1916 with the host side winning 20-9.

The inauguration, in 1917, of the Forsyth Shield competition gave an added impetus to the growth of Rugby Union at Duntroon. This annual event between representative teams from Sydney's Great Public Schools

Officers of the 1st Battalion (New South Wales) outside their tents at Mena Camp, Egypt, during training, March 1915. Sitting on the left in the back row is Major Blair Swannell, a Rugby Union international who, according to one witness, had 'his head half blown off' on the day of the Gallipoli landings. Also killed that day was the man sitting in front of Swannell, Lieutenant William Duchesne. Next to Swannell sits Lieutenant Alfred Shout, who received the Victoria Cross for bravery at Lone Pine, but died on 11 August 1915 of wounds received in the fighting. Captain Harold Jacobs, seated in front on the right, was the only one to survive the war.

AWM C02130

and the United Services (RMC and RANC) provided important opportunities for cadets to test their skills in a wide range of arenas.

In 1917 the match against Navy was played at Duntroon before a large crowd that included Brigadier General

Parnell and staff, Mr W. W. Hill, the secretary of the NSW Rugby Union, prominent local identities and a contingent of ladies. The match was refereed by Captain Broadbent and from the opening kick-off play was 'fast, open, and interesting.' The final result was a decided victory for Duntroon 47-nil. Similar results were recorded in 1918 (RMC 33-RANC nil) and 1919 (RMC 99-RANC nil).

Not surprisingly, the raising of the Australian Imperial Force (AIF) attracted a significant number of Rugby Union players to the ranks and press reports from early 1915 frequently contain detailed information about enlistments from NSW and Queensland metropolitan and country clubs alike. At home the NSW and Metropolitan Rugby Unions decided 'to play only a limited number of fixtures and devote the time thus gained to the training of its players, ex-players, officials and supporters for military purposes.' The scheme for military drill gained support in Sydney and outlying districts as the Rugby Union association became a driving force behind recruitment of sportsmen from clubs and local associations.

From the beginning of the First World War campaigns at Gallipoli in 1915 through to the years on the Western Front, Rugby Union became well established itself as a popular pastime for AIF footballers and an integral part of army sporting events between units of the AIF and of course, against the New Zealanders and British in particular. In Egypt army Rugby Union flourished with most units of the AIF containing players who were well known in their home states:

> Mr. W. W. Hill, secretary of the New South Wales Rugby Union, has received word from Egypt that a match under Rugby Union rules was played there last month between New Zealand and New South Wales, the former winning by 24 to 17. There were eight players on the winning side who had previously played with a Dominion representative side, while seven New South Wales Blues figured with the losers...

Later Hill's brother in Cairo wrote that: 'The New South Wales Brigade and its attached units have been playing inter-brigade and inter-unit matches', most of which were held 'on beautiful flat land at the foot of the Cheops Pyramid'. From these games it was the Army Medical Corps that 'emerged victorious'.

Of course AIF personnel in England for training, medical recuperation or posted to AIF depots there quickly engaged with local British Army and civilian teams. For example, in April 1916 a team of Australian soldiers played a match against a team representing the North of England at Headingly, Leeds. A crowd of twelve thousand spectators saw the Australians defeated by just two points on the 'well-appointed ground of the Leeds Northern Union Club.' The Australian soldiers were received with enormous enthusiasm and entertained at a civic dinner hosted by Leeds' Lord Mayor. Proceeds from the event were distributed to war charities.

March 1917 saw a match between a team from AIF Headquarters (HQ) London and the Wanderers, with AIF HQ victorious 44-3. A year later AIF HQ played the NZ Convalescent Hospital (a draw) and played the NZ HQ (a loss 3-11). An Army team also played crew from HMAS *Australia* in September 1917, reflecting an Army-Navy competitiveness also being played out at home between RMC and RANC that year.

In fact there were so many matches going on in England, principally involving the AIF HQ, that a comparison with the match opportunities on the Western Front could not have been starker as the soldiers at the front fought, rested or labored, only being able to play in the main impromptu or intra-unit matches. Between October 1917 and November 1918 alone, matches were played in England against the Welsh Guards, NZ HQ, Greater Public Schools, Royal Aircraft Factory, Royal Naval Depot, Aldershot Command Group, NZ Field Artillery, Canadian HQ, Royal Flying Corps, NZ Convalescent Hospital, the British Army Service Corps, British Army Motor Transport Corps, Haileybury College, Cardiff and the Pill Harriers Club from South Wales, among others.

We know from photographic evidence alone that Rugby Union was played at all levels and all types of units, including fighting units of the AIF whether in France or the Middle East. Australian soldiers loved their sport, and being close to the front line wasn't going to stop them from having a good match of Rugby Union, among other sports.

The AIF HQ team was to remain a fixture of the Rugby Union scene for the AIF throughout the war, even though it would have seen constant turnover in players. On the Western Front, divisional teams came together to form an AIF 'Trench' team to play against the French Army.

With the end of the War, a new period of intense Rugby Union competition asserted itself in both France and England, in part to keep the AIF personnel active and engaged while they awaited repatriation to Australia. The Trench Team and the AIF Headquarters team were to come together to form the famous 1919 AIF Rugby Union teams.

The 59th Battalion playing rugby football behind the line at Barleux. Identified is 5196 Private W. R. Saunders (holding the ball, second from right, foreground). 20 September 1918
AWM E05533

The Rugby Union Team of the 116th Howitzer Battery, Australian Imperial Force.
Private Collection

Kick-off–
The 1919 Australian
Imperial Force
Rugby Union Teams

With the end of hostilities on 11 November 1918 Army authorities were keen to ensure that all members of the AIF were appropriately occupied. Shipping was scarce and the leaders of the AIF were keen not to undermine the reputation of the AIF with ill-disciplined behaviour which might occur as the troops waited to go home. The emphasis was on encouraging participation in all forms of healthy sport during the immediate post-Armistice period and opportunities were developed for participation in a wide range of competitions, with Rugby Union in the lead.

Initially, much of the organization of these events occurred under the leadership of the 19th Battalion's Major S. A. Middleton, Distinguished Service Order, who had a tremendous reputation in both rowing and Rugby Union. A flurry of inter-battalion, inter-brigade, inter-division and corps competitions in France, Belgium, England and the Middle East got underway.

In January 1919 these competitions became more formalized when the AIF established a Sports Control Board, responsible for organising sports including Rugby Union, Australian Rules football, 'association football' (soccer), cross-country running, boxing, rowing, and rifle shooting among others. Middleton was appointed Organising Secretary and the Australian Comforts Fund guaranteed the major portion of the cost.

In accordance with an arrangement made some time previously with representatives of the French Rugby Union, in early 1919 a group of between sixty and seventy Rugby Union players, selected from the AIF, was brought together in order to choose an AIF team to play the French Army in Paris.

As there had not been enough time to conduct test matches each Division had been asked to submit the names its eight best players. Team selection for the match in Paris on 19 January 1919 was made after two weeks of training at a special school near the Belgian village of Barbencon.

This side, known as the 'Trench' Team, was coached by Jim Clarken and 'Munnie' Fraser. Major W. F. 'Wally' Matthews, a well-known pre-war Sydney University player was selected to manage the AIF team which went on to win the match in Paris 6-3.

At the conclusion of the match, the team left for England where it met the AIF Headquarters Team and played some other local matches. It was from the Trench Team and the AIF Headquarters Team that the AIF First XV and Reserve XV for the Inter-Service Rugby Union Competition in England, and the awarding of the King's Cup, was selected.

Selected as captain of the AIF First XV was Lieutenant W. T. 'Bill' Watson, Military Cross and Bar, Distinguished Conduct Medal, while Peter Buchanan from the Trench Team captained the Australian Reserves Team. Under the leadership of Major Matthews, the AIF teams developed a wonderful spirit of camaraderie, becoming immensely popular and successful.

At the same time, an Australian Corps competition also got underway in France, with teams from each of the Divisions and one from Corps troops; 2nd Division came out on top. Conditions did not deter the players:

> ... the grounds were not by any means ideal. One day a game would be played on a field covered in a couple of inches of snow. At another time the snow would give place to a similar depth of mud, and yet again the ground would be frozen hard...the teams often had to undertake journeys of between [20] and [30] kilometers—and even more—over bumpy roads, and return after the game. The Army wagon was not by any means a well-upholstered or well-sprung conveyance, and it had no central heating arrangements ...

A combined Corps team was then chosen to represent the 4th Army against a 2nd Army (British) team, which they defeated in a match in Cologne. The team also played a match against the Royal Air Force, which it defeated handily.

The Inter-Service and Dominion Forces Rugby Union Competition commenced in England on 1 March 1919. In addition to Australia, teams from Canada, New Zealand, South Africa, the Royal Air Force and Great

The Australian 'Trench' rugby football team which defeated the AIF Headquarters by twelve points to six.

Back row, left to right: Gunner James Hamilton Bosward, 5th Field Artillery Brigade (FAB); Lieutenant (Lt) Cody; Sapper Dunn; Driver James Clarken 4th AMTS; Sergeant (Sgt) Bradley; Lt William Charles O'Toole, 2nd Pioneer Battalion; Lt William Thornton Watson MC & Bar DCM, 2nd FAB.

Middle row: Private (Pte) Lyons; Sgt Suttor; Pte Leahy; Company Sergeant Major Buchanan, captain; Captain Beith; Pte Stephenson; Pte Thompson.

Front row: Pte Flanaghan; Quartermaster Sergeant Bond.

AWM D002260

The Australian Imperial Force First XV Rugby Union Team, 1919.
Private Collection

Britain (referred to as the 'Mother Country') competed. The Australian teams—both firsts and reserves—trained at Chiswick Park in London. Journeying from their headquarters to Leicester, the Australian team played its first match against the Mother Country on 8 March 1919.

Contemporary accounts of the AIF Team's inaugural match note that; 'although the match was "an evenly contested one, the AIF team suffered from an obvious 'lack of combined effort"'. The outcome, before a crowd of nine thousand, was a victory for the Mother Country 6-3. Successive matches were scheduled against: South Africa at Newport on 15 March, NZ at Bradford on 22 March, the Royal Air Force at Gloucester on 29 March and Canada at Twickenham on 5 April. Headquartered in London, about fifty players were provided with board and accommodation and transport to their matches.

The team selected to play at Newport on 15 March 1919 was somewhat different from the Leicester team in that Sergeant Bradley and Private Quinn took the places of Thompson and Murray in the forwards, while the playing coach, 'Wally' Matthews, worked behind the scrum in place of Buchanan, and Poutney and Bosward came in as centre three-quarters. The Australians won the match 8-5, Suttor and Bradley being the scorers with Stenning converting the try of Suttor.

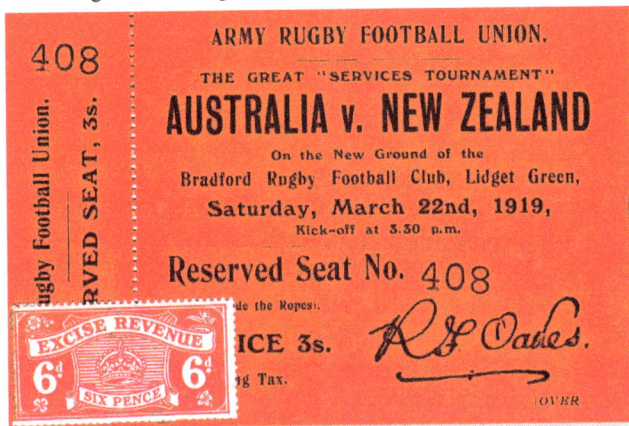

A Ticket for the Australia versus New Zealand Match of 22 March 1919.

Private Collection

The postponement of the match against the NZ side due to three inches of snow on the field meant that the next AIF match was against the Royal Air Force. Changes to the AIF team included the selection of Egan in the three-quarter line to replace an injured Stenning, and Thompson to the forwards in place of Quinn. The result was not a good one for the AIF Team which lost to the Air Force 7-3.

The match against Canada at Twickenham on 5 April was attended by both the Prince of Wales and Prince Albert and it was in this match that the Australians 'played really first-class football for the first time.' The final score of 38-nil was a testament to the player's individual skills and excellent team work and demonstrated the depth of talent that existed within the ranks of the Australian Forces. At the conclusion of the match the Princes came onto the field to speak to the players.

By this stage of the competition, NZ had won all their four matches and the Mother Country three. It only remained for NZ to defeat the Australians in their match at Bradford and the cup to be presented by the King would be theirs. However, to the surprise of many, the rapidly-improving Australian XV won the match on 9 April with the tight score of 6-5. For the Australians, this was the end of the competition and NZ went on to defeat the Mother Country for the King's Cup. The beginning of the competition had seen considerable adverse criticism of the 'rough methods employed by the Australian team.' However, as the contest progressed the criticism abated and press reports congratulated the players on the positive spirit in which the matches were played.

The publicity surrounding the competition for the King's Cup tended to overshadow the extensive program of Rugby Union matches played throughout England and

Wales and around London during the early months of 1919. The energy and drive of team manager, Lieutenant L. W. Seaborn, MC, contributed to the success of the Reserve Team, while Major Matthews' fine record with the First XV continued with matches against:

- The Australian Flying Corps, 15 February at Gloucester. First XV won 50-nil.
- The South African Army Team, 19 February at Queen's Club. First XV won 9-8.
- Leicester County, 22 February at Leicester. Win 8-6.
- NZ Army A Team, 26 February at Richmond. Loss 9-nil.
- Devon County, 12 April at Exeter. Win 11-3.
- Royal Naval Depot, 16 April at Plymouth. Win 14-10.
- Maesteg, 19 April at Maesteg. Loss 18-3.
- Pill Harriers, 21 April at Newport. Loss 12-3.
- Abertillery, 23 April at Abertillery. Win 11-3.
- Ogmore Vale, 26 April at Ogmore Vale. Loss 6-3.
- Cornwall, 3 May at Penzance. Win 9-nil.

At the same time, the Reserve Team also established a fine reputation as a Rugby Union force to be reckoned with, having been responsible for breaking a long-held record when they became the first team to defeat Llanelly on their own ground on 15 March 1919. The success of the Reserve Team can be seen from the results of matches against:

- AIF Depot, 15 February at Warminster. Win 19-10.
- 18th Wing RAF, 19 February at Hounslow. Win 52-nil.

- AIF Depots, 22 February at Warminster. Win 8-3.
- NZ Army B Team, 26 February at Richmond. Loss 17-3.
- Guy's Hospital, 8 March at Chiswick. Win 25-nil.
- Llanelly, 15 March at Llanelly. Win 11-nil.
- East Midlands, 29 March at Northhampton. Win 27-11.
- Llanelly, 12 April at Llanelly. Loss 11-8.
- Exmouth, 19 April at Exeter. Win 21-3.
- Devon County, 21 April at Newton Abbott. Win 21-3.
- Teignmouth, 23 April at Teignmouth. Win 40-3.
- Llanelly, 3 May at Llanelly. Loss 17-3.

The teams left England in May, arriving in Australia on the RMS *Orontes* at the beginning of July to great public acclaim. The team manager Major Matthews, team captain Lieutenant W. T. Watson and the thirty-five members of what was by now a well-known and popular military and sporting entity were welcomed by a large gathering of Rugby Union enthusiasts that included the secretary of the NSW Rugby Union. The next day the team enjoyed more accolades at an official government welcome held at the Australia Hotel and later that night enjoyed a night out at the theatre, having been invited to attend the J.C. Williamson production of *Goody Two Shoes*.

On Saturday 5 July 1919, before a crowd of ten thousand, the returned men played a representative NSW team—a match preceded by a match between the AIF Reserve XV team and a NSW Second XV,

The Australian Imperial Force Reserve XV Rugby Union Team, 1919.
Private Collection

which NSW won 25-11. The Union arranged for school children and returned soldiers 'with badges' to be admitted free to the game and made special arrangements for 'wounded men from the military hospitals'. A comprehensive report of the first division match (NSW was soundly defeated 42-14) in the *Sydney Morning Herald* went on to highlight the outstanding record achieved by the AIF teams in Britain and France:

'...the Diggers thoroughly deserved the high reputation that had preceded them', and went on to say: '...the fifteen stands out as one of the greatest seen on Sydney grounds'.

The news report also drew attention to the impact the war had had on Rugby Union. About five thousand Rugby Union players had joined the AIF and of these more than five hundred had been killed in action. The loss of so many players and increasing competition from the Rugby League code saw some question whether the game would survive. However, the paper also pointed out that the return of Rugby Union players from military service overseas and the strength of the game at Duntroon and the RANC meant that its survival was pretty much ensured.

The following Saturday 12 July, at the University Oval, the AIF team played an Australian team chosen from NSW and Queensland, defeating it 28-18. The next day they visited the 'garden suburb for soldiers at Matraville' where they labored for most of the day on various improvement projects:

> Stiff and sore from their exertions on the previous afternoon members of the A.I.F. Rugby Union team were early visitors to the garden suburb for soldiers at Matraville yesterday. Arming themselves with long handled shovels they spent a strenuous morning, and after being refreshed by luncheon returned to the attack in the afternoon. It had been expected that the team which represented Australia on Saturday against the Diggers would co-operate with the latter in assaulting a sand hill, but their absence was explained by more or less general exhaustion.

On 15 July 1919 the team played a New England side in Armidale defeating it 35-11, before travelling to Brisbane where they defeated Queensland 38-7 on 19 July in front of a crowd of around five thousand spectators. On 23 July the team played a Queensland AIF team (which included some of their own Reserve XV team) on the Brisbane Cricket Ground and defeated them as well, 30-3. On 26 July they played again against Australia at the Brisbane Cricket Ground and defeated the joint Queensland-NSW team 20-13.

On their way back to Sydney they played the North Western Association side on the Showground in Inverell, defeating it 52-6. They completed their tour by defeating Australia once again by 22-6 on 2 August at the Sydney Sports Ground. It was their last match, and the weary but triumphant veterans disbanded, their war finally over.

This final match of these unique AIF teams of 'comrades in arms and in sport' marked the end of what had been a hugely successful series of matches and heralded a re-vitalisation of the game of Rugby Union in NSW and Queensland. It was remarkable that the AIF veterans still had the capacity for tough and vigorous play after the basic diet, privation, stress and difficulties faced by them during active service. The younger men who faced them on the Rugby Union field upon their return to Sydney faced not just physically tough men but men who had played on bigger and more lethal battlefields.

While some continued to play club Rugby Union immediately after the war, most had given their all and were content to rest at last. The AIF team coach and manager, Wally Matthews, stayed on to manage the 1933 Wallaby team tour of South Africa while the team captain, Billy Watson, went on to win a Distinguished Service Order at Kokoda in WWII.

Spectators gather on the field after the Army rugby football match between New Zealand and Australia at Bradford, the Australians being the winners by six points to five. 9 April 1919.

AWM D00532

The 9th Australian Light Horse, AIF, Rugby Union Team (known as the Kangaroos) in England, 1919.
AWM H01895

The Rugby Union Team of the 4th Australian Machine Gun Company.
AWM H02436

Outstanding on the Field— the First World War Era Greats

About five thousand Rugby Union players enlisted in the AIF during the First World War, and more than 500 were killed in action. Among the most notable of the players who survived the First World War were those men who formed the great 1919 AIF teams. No less than 14 from the two teams were Wallabies, one was a Waratah and one was even a Kangaroo. Remarkably, one member won gold medals in Rugby Union at the Olympics for both Australia and the USA.

Lieutenant William 'Billy' Thornton Watson (1887-1961)

Lieutenant 'Billy' Watson, Military Cross and Bar, Distinguished Conduct Medal was the team captain of the 1919 side. He later won a Distinguished Service Order on the Kokoda Track in World War II (the Second World War). Born in New Zealand, Watson came to Australia before the First World War and settled in Sydney with his Victorian wife. He was selected for the Waratahs of 1912 and the Australian tour of the USA and Canada that year. He toured NZ in 1913 and also represented Australia in the All Blacks tour of Australia in 1914. With the outbreak of the First World War, Watson enlisted

William Watson

on 8 August 1914 and served with the Australian Naval and Military Expeditionary Force and took part in operations in New Britain and New Ireland.

He then joined the AIF and served as a gunner at Gallipoli and the Western Front. Sergeant Watson was awarded the Distinguished Conduct Medal at the Somme in January 1917, and was commissioned in September. He was wounded in Belgium in November, recovered and went on to win a Military Cross in August 1918 and a Bar to the Military Cross in October, when he was also gassed.

Watson was tough—he then captained the AIF First XV team right through its matches in England and Australia in 1919. When playing in Australia with the AIF team as a front-row forward, Watson must have suffered excruciating pain as he was covered in festering sores, the after-effects of mustard gas. Major Walter 'Wally' Matthews, the team manager, frequently had to open these festering sores with a sterilised penknife before Watson took to the field.

In 1920 Watson captained NSW against NZ. Working in the United States between the wars, Watson returned to Australia when the Second World War broke out. He served with the 2nd Australian Garrison Battalion. Posted to the Papuan Infantry Battalion, where he became the commanding officer, Watson fought at Kokoda and was awarded the Distinguished Service Order. Promoted to major, Watson remained on operations in New Guinea until mid-1944. After the war he became Australian vice-consul in New York until 1952. Watson was a great leader, a great Rugby Union player and a great Australian.

Dudley 'Dud' Colin Suttor (1892–1962)

Another remarkable player was 'Dud' Suttor. Suttor was born in country NSW. He represented NSW in Rugby Union in 1912 and just missed selection in the Australian team which toured the United States that year. Bathurst was so upset over his omission that the city immediately swung its support over to Rugby League. A comment on Suttor in 1912 was:

> Suttor, the left wing three quarter back was the crackerjack player of the side. He scored three brilliant tries and would have scored three dozen had J. Flynn never been born.

Dudley Suttor

Suttor as a winger is the ideal, a man who shoots off the mark like lead out of a Winchester, fast as a Zebra, and generally, a reckless, daring smashing player.

Suttor toured NZ as a wing three quarter with the 1913 Waratahs and earned his international cap. He was leading try getter on the tour with seven tries. Enlisting in the AIF in June 1915, Suttor was a driver with the 15th Australian Army Service Corps. He saw service in Egypt, France and Belgium.

In 1919, chosen as a member of the AIF Trench Team, Suttor joined other Western Front Australian players at a School of Physical and Recreational Training, near Barbencon, in Belgium, to train for a match against the French Army in Paris, which the Australians won 6-3.

The AIF Trench Team then went on a football tour of England, playing various teams and the AIF Headquarters Team (defeating them 12 to 6).

Suttor was then chosen for the 1919 AIF First XV Team, and played in all the matches of the English championship and subsequent Australian tour. One press comment in Australia was:

> The final between the Diggers and Our Boys resulted in a ding dong struggle during the first half, but in the second spell the fighting boys with a brisk breeze behind them, charged the line repeatedly, and had all the best of the game. Suttor electrified the shivering barrackers with his dashing sprints goal wards...

> Ever the sportsman, and excellent swimmer and body surfer, Dudley Suttor passed away in 1962 aged 70 years whilst competing in a 55 yard Returned and Services League swimming race at the Dee Why pool.

Daniel Brendon Carroll (1892–1956)

Lieutenant Daniel Brendon Carroll, Distinguished Service Cross (United States Army) was an Australian national representative Rugby Union player. He was a dual Olympic gold medalist winning in Rugby Union at the 1908 Summer Olympics for Australia and also winning gold for the United States at the 1920 Summer Olympics. He later coached the gold-medal winning USA Rugby Union team at the 1924 Summer Olympics.

Carroll was born at Flemington, Victoria. His family relocated to Sydney during his childhood. He played

Rugby Union with St Aloysius' College in the school's First XV and then at Sydney University; his club Rugby Union was played with St George. Carroll was a winger at that time; later in his career he played at fly-half.

He was selected in Australia's inaugural national rugby team to tour the northern hemisphere—Dr Paddy Moran's first Wallabies team for the 1908-09 Australia Rugby Union tour of the British Isles and France. He was the youngest member of the tour squad at 20 years. Carroll played as a winger in the first Test of the tour, the 6-9 loss to Wales at Cardiff Arms Park, which was the first Rugby Union Test played by an Australian team on British soil.

The Wallabies went on to an easy 32-3 victory over Cornwall (representing England) in the Olympics. Each Wallaby in that match became an Olympic gold medallist; Carroll scored two tries. In 1912 he was again selected in the Wallabies squad to tour the USA and Canada, but the hospitality played havoc with team discipline—the team lost against two California University sides and three Canadian provincial sides.

They rose to the occasion for the sole Test of the tour—the November 1912 clash against the United States at Berkeley, won 12-8. Carroll played at fly-half in that match and scored a try. Carroll thus made two Test career appearances for Australia. Carroll stayed on in America after the 1912 tour.

He played for All-America against the All Blacks in 1913, a Test won by NZ 51-3. He served in the American

Daniel Carroll

Army as a Lieutenant in the First World War and was awarded a Distinguished Service Cross. In 1919 he was 'co-opted' into the Australian AIF Rugby Union team and played two matches for the First XV, against Canada and NZ, in the international tournament in England.

He completed a degree in geology at Stanford University in 1920 and was coaching Rugby Union at the university when he was selected as the playing coach of the USA side selected for the 1920 Summer Olympics. He won a gold medal at Antwerp in that team playing at fly-half.

Carroll made three Rugby Union Test career appearances for the United States between 1913 and 1920. One report has Carroll playing four years of Rugby

Union at Stanford and one year of American football. He won his letter in Rugby Union in 1913, 1914 and 1915. He played his last match of Rugby Union in 1921 when a pick-up team visited British Columbia.

After Stanford, Carroll furthered his education at Oxford and the Royal School of Mines in England. In 1921 he took up an appointment with Standard Oil and remained with the company until his retirement. However, his non-playing Rugby Union career continued when in 1924, he was coach of the US team which won gold again at the Paris Olympics.

Dr Walter 'Wally' Fredrick Matthews (1884-1954)

A key administrator (and player) was Dr 'Wally' Matthews. Matthews played Rugby Union for NSW in 1906, 1908 and 1910 and was considered unlucky not to gain selection in the Wallaby team of 1908.

At the end of the First World War, the then Major Matthews was in England and the AIF Sports Control Board appointed him as team manager for the 1919 AIF Rugby Union team, which toured England before touring undefeated in Australia. Matthews continued his close association with the game on his return to Australia.

In 1933 he was paid the great honour of being selected as Tour Manager for the Wallabies team to South Africa. This team was generally considered to be the first Australian team to make a tour to a major Rugby Union nation with a truly Australian representation.

Dr Walter Matthews

The team played 23 matches on its South Africa tour, winning 12, drawing one and losing 10, and caused an upset after early poor form to defeat the Springboks in two tests. Matthews became one of Orange's most respected sporting administrators, having an enormous influence on both cricket and Rugby Union in the district. He was also Mayor of Orange from 1936-1944 and 1948-1950. In 1937 the visiting Springboks played in Orange and South African tour manager, Percy Day, said that on the 1933 tour Dr Matthews proved to be one of the most popular Australia sportsmen to visit South Africa.

Play Continues–
Australian Army
Rugby Union 1920-
1952

In the immediate post-First World War period, the Army shrank back to a small rump of disparate parts—a small Permanent Army, a larger but skeletal Militia and a small Reserve. The Australian economy remained depressed. Within the decade, and with the crash on Wall Street banks in October 1929, a world-wide depression began which caused unemployment in Australia to hit 35% by 1931. The economy had barely started to recover a decade later when the Second World War intervened. It was not until the 1950s that the Australian economy began to boom once more 'on the sheep's back.'

After the grand success of the 1919 AIF Rugby Union teams, and with the disbandment of the AIF itself, in the 1920s the Royal Military College kept the Army Rugby Union flame burning. Unit teams played throughout the country at large, including the non-traditional Rugby Union states such as Western Australia, South Australia, Victoria and Tasmania.

One effect during the first half of the post-war decade was a decrease in cadet numbers at Duntroon. In 1920 it was also decided that the competition would be more even if players were of a similar age. The result was, that Duntroon agreed to field a team drawn from the Third and Fourth classes, which meant that during the 1920s both sides recorded wins.

Against a background of the depression of the early 1930s, the Royal Military College found itself temporarily relocated to Sydney's Victoria Barracks in 1931. Despite a lack of suitable sporting facilities at the Barracks, cadets soon found the availability of local teams meant increasing opportunities for competition. In the six years the College was in Sydney, RMC's First XV played around eighteen matches each season, establishing a reputation as an outstanding exponent of the game.

In 1931 and 1932 RMC participated in the competition for the Kentwell Cup. From 1933 until its return to Canberra in 1937, the cadets distinguished themselves against public and government school teams, the Hawkesbury River Agricultural College and local army and navy teams.

In its first year back in Canberra, the College won the Forsayth Shield and played a series of matches against visiting rugby teams from Sydney. 1937 also saw the scheduling of a match between the visiting South African Springboks and the College—unfortunately cancelled due to an outbreak of German measles. The following year RMC Duntroon joined the Australian Capital Territory Rugby Union Competition and by 1939 was fielding a team in the senior grade and another in the lightweight grade—winning the premiership by defeating Canberra's Eastern Suburbs in the final.

In Western Australia, an Army team was playing in reserve grade by 1931, a year when Army also played against teams from HMAS *Australia*. By 1933, the Army's Artillery Rugby Union Club had become a United Services team and had a place on the First Grade championship ladder. No doubt many of them watched Western Australia play the Wallabies *en route* to their South African tour in May 1933. In South Australia, an Army team debuted in the local competition in 1935; by 1938, they were second on the premiership ladder. Matches against the South Australian Navy team also continued the traditional rivalry between the two services started at RMC in 1917.

In Victoria, a Citizen Force team from the 37th and 52nd Battalions was entered into a 10-strong First Grade competition, along with Navy and Air Force teams. The success of Army and other service teams was so prominent by 1937, that a separate service competition for teams representing the Air Force and Militia was promoted by Victorian Rugby Union. A cup valued at more than £100 was made available for perpetual competition among the Service teams. It was even suggested that the competition be arranged as a curtain-raiser to the Inter-state and South African matches to be played in Melbourne in June.

Even in Tasmania, Army was strong enough by 1938 to field a side in both First and Second Grade competitions. In New South Wales, a strong Artillery team had been encouraged by Lieutenant-Colonel G.W.F. Meredith, Officer-in-Charge of the First Heavy Brigade of the Royal Australian Artillery (RAA). By 1939, its success was sufficiently recognised to seek entry into the NSW First Grade District Competition. Its application was refused by NSW Rugby Union on the basis that the team lists were full. NSW Rugby Union suggested an inter-services competition instead, and Army had to be content with continuing in the Sub-District competition, where it played for the Burke Cup.

At the same time, many of the Artillery Club men from North Head represented Army in the Inter-Services matches of 1939, in which the Army wore a scarlet jersey. From the triangular series, a Service XV team was chosen

A rugby union match between Australians and South African soldiers in Beirut, Syria, 1942.

AWM 024231

to play the Metropolitan Colts XV team in August 1939; all of the Army members were from the RAA. In the supporting fixture, the RAA's Second XV from the Metropolitan Sub-District competition (where it was leading the table) played Christian Brothers.

In Queensland, Rugby Union was the poor relation of the dominant Rugby League code. In the immediate post-First World War period, Rugby Union could not even hold a senior competition, such was the dearth of interest after the highlight of the visit of the 1919 AIF Team, and it wasn't until 1926 that Rugby Union was 're-established'. By 1932, 10,000 spectators watched NSW defeat Queensland 9-8, but it was not until 1937 that the newspapers record an Army team playing a Navy team at Gregory Terrace in Brisbane. While no doubt some unit Rugby Union was being played, Army Rugby Union in Queensland remained a 'poor cousin' compared to competitions in other States.

The outbreak of war in September 1939 did not unduly curtail sporting activities at Duntroon. Sport was regarded as a vital part of the overall training program and therefore Rugby Union continued essentially unchanged. While it was more difficult to organize matches against external teams, cadets had many opportunities to participate in intra-collegiate matches, particularly against the officers' training wing. Though the traditional Forsayth Shield Rugby Union match was not held in 1940, it resumed in 1941 and continued

Group portrait of allied prisoners of war (POWs) who made up the Fort 15 Rugby Union team at Stalag XXa, a German POW and internment camp circa 1942.
Included in the photo are Warrant Officer Class 2 K. L. Winton Healey (middle row, fourth from left), the team's coach, and Dave Uhr (front row, far right).
AWM P02071.018

throughout the war with RMC Duntroon winning in 1941, 1942, 1943 and 1946.

In 1945 the question of competing football codes (Australian Rules and Rugby Union) caused some controversy when a West Australian senator asked why cadets were not permitted to play Australian Rules. The official response from Duntroon not only argued that Rugby Union was the game played in the areas most cadets came from, but that much of the standing of the College was associated with the success of its Rugby Union teams— considered to be amongst the best in the nation.

Following the end of the war in 1945 cadet numbers began to increase and by 1950 Duntroon had three Rugby Union grounds and four teams. Rugby Union was going from strength to strength. Forsayth Shield matches continued—though not without controversy surrounding the ages and abilities of the cadets compared with the Sydney school boys.

In other parts of the Army, Rugby Union was revitalised by wartime preparation and activity, as club and representative Rugby Union players enlisted in the services. In Sydney, AIF teams were selected to play Metropolitan teams in a fund-raiser matches for Patriotic Funds in August 1940, while an AIF team from Redbank Camp in Brisbane played Queensland in August 1940. Unit and formation teams, with artillery teams prominent, were formed and inter-unit sport was given especial emphasis as Australians trained for war. These matches often had Australian, State and First Grade club players in them.

With the despatch of the Second AIF overseas, a replay of the 1919 Paris match against the French Army was played out in Beirut, in then Syria, on 28th April 1940. The AIF team was selected following a Possibles vs. Probables exhibition match in Tel Aviv in Palestine the week before. Seven thousand spectators saw the AIF Team defeat the French Army champion team, *the Marsouins*, 11-5, after the French led 5-3 at half-time.

The Australians wore a green jersey with a gold rising sun on the chest, although other reports stated a royal blue jersey was worn. The Australian team comprised Maxwell,

A rugby union match between the 2/1st Australian Tank Attack Regiment and the 61st Australian Infantry Battalion in Donadabu, PNG, 1943.

AWM 057069

Frank Hassett—a former RMC player—McElhone, Movicker, Richard Feather-stonehaugh, (Captain) Basil 'Jika' Travers, and W. H. Travers, Leslie Matchett and Wand, Long, Campbell, Louis Loughran, Dunbar, Donald Jackson—a former RMC player—and (vice-captain) Edward 'Weary' Dunlop.

On the eve of the match, Travers said that the team had not had as much training as would normally be considered necessary for such an important game, but every player was fit and keen. "We are meeting a team which has many internationals in it," he said, "but I am confident that the French Army will not have a walk-over. I believe they play a fast, open match, which should suit our Australian play."

During the war, Rugby Union matches were played everywhere, at home and abroad. Prior to the military defeat of the Allied Forces in Singapore at the hands of the Japanese, the Singapore-Johore Rugby Union team, sprinkled with leading Australian Service players, including two Wallabies now with the AIF, defeated the British Army team 16-5. In February 1941, a 42-team, seven-aside tournament took place at Alexandria in Egypt, in which four Australian teams (two from the AIF) took part. In January 1942 the New Zealanders defeated the AIF side at Gezirah in Egypt, the 'enzeds' winning 11-3, although 'both sides were suffering from the effects of an extra-large helping of Christmas "duff".

Matches continued in Australia between Commands, formations and units. In Western Australia, Army Rugby Union flourished under Major General Horace C.H. Robertson (founder of the ACT Rugby Union and better known as 'Red Robbie') in a competition with 43 unit teams. These included a winning Armoured Brigade team among others, including two American teams. In June 1944, an Army XV played New South Wales—players included the 1941 AIF team captain from Beirut, Captain Basil. H. 'Jika' Travers:

> A visit to the Army Rugby team's camp at the Showground revealed that the Army men in training, in typical "Aussie" style, are already "cobbers" in the best sense. Rank counts for nothing as the men eat, sleep and play together—officer, "non-com" and private alike....the Old A.I.F. won a reputation on account of their magnificent physique, but the 1944 A.I.F. forwards will dwarf the former Anzacs...

In the wake of the Second World War, Rugby Union continued but perhaps without the same intensity without the 'name' players, who were returning to their clubs and State sides. A mid-week union of 17 teams was revived in Sydney in early 1946 which included an Army team. In 1946 a New South Wales United Services side toured Victoria. In 1948, a South Australian Army side defeated Victoria. RMC again won the ACT First Grade premiership in 1949. In 1950 Army played teams from the Eastern Suburbs Rugby Union Club in Sydney, while Western Suburbs played a United Services side in 1950. Meanwhile, competition between the three services for the Stan McCabe Cup continued.

Overseas, in the British Commonwealth Occupation Force (BCOF) in Japan and in Korea,

The Army XV in the Inter-service Competition
for the Stan McCabe Cup in 1945.
AWM 114888

Rugby Union also flourished. One infantry captain wrote:

> In the Occupation Force rugby is very popular, the main drawback being the lack of good grounds. Many games are played on unit parade grounds, which usually have no grass on them whatsoever. Even small gravel rashes soon fester, and poisoned limbs are quite common. This seldom dampens interest though.

A unique competition took place in the BCOF when teams from Australia, Britain, New Zealand and India competed for the Duntroon Cup, presented by graduates of RMC Duntroon on duty with the BCOF. The competition and cup was the idea of the Commander-in-Chief of the BCOF, Australia's Lieutenant-General H. C. H. Robertson.

From Korea, Australia and New Zealand Army teams played in a match organised in Japan. It appeared that the Australian team was comprised of RMC graduates including Maj. J.W. Norrie (formerly coach at RMC), Lt. R. Grey (1951), Capt. B. Trenerry (1944), Lt. F. C. Smith (1951), Lt. R. Hutton (1950), Lt. A. L. Limburg (1951), Lt. J. W. Black (1951), Maj. R. Sutton (1942). Lieutenant Colin Nadar Kahn (1951) led the RMC Rugby Union team in 1951 and was a Canberra representative in Rugby Union. As captain of Scots College team he represented the Greater Public Schools against RMC in 1947, and four years later he played for Duntroon against GPS. He was seriously wounded in Korea, but would retain a lifelong interest in the game.

Group portrait of the 34th Infantry Brigade Rugby Union Team in the Meiji Stadium, Japan, 1947.

Team Captain Sergeant (Sgt) Joseph Bede Patrick O'Sullivan in middle row, far right.

Sgt O'Sullivan from Berrima, NSW, enlisted in May 1940 aged 22. He was to spend the next 32 years in the army, seeing service with the 2/13th Battalion during the Second World War in North Africa, New Guinea and Borneo. He served with the British Commonwealth Occupation Force in Japan (BCOF) and later in Korea and Malaya. In 1962 he was made an MBE; he retired as a Warrant Officer Class 1 in 1972.

AWM P10310.002

The Golden Years of Duntroon Rugby Union 1911-1963

Rugby Union Honour Cap awarded to Cadet Officer Norman Clowes, Royal Military College, Duntroon 1913-1914.

The Royal Military College Duntroon, at least until 1986 when the Australian Defence Force Academy superceded it in Rugby Union terms, has led the way for Army Rugby Union from its emergence as Duntroon's principal football code soon after the establishment of the College in 1911. Some of the best players to join Army Rugby Union, Joint Service and in some cases, Australian teams over the years have been 'graduates' from the Rugby Union nursery at Duntroon, where Rugby Union was seen as an essential part of the training curriculum.

Although there had been heated discussions about the code of football that would be played by College cadets at the start-up of the College, the decision in favour of Rugby Union was strongly influenced by the game's pre-eminent position in New South Wales and Canberra at that time. Rugby Union at Duntroon went on to have many highlights over the years of play, but perhaps this golden age of the game at RMC was exemplified by the cadet teams of 1954-55, which defeated not just the Greater Public Schools XV but also the highly regarded Sydney City Colts. In 1962, RMC again won, but for the last time, the ACT First Grade premiership.

Duntroon's first Rugby Union club was established by V.J.R. Miles, the professor of English, and on 15 July 1911 the First XV played its inaugural match against the local Queanbeyan team, the Warrigals (losing 12-nil). That year there were two more matches played against visiting sides and a total of seven games in 1912. By 1913, a total of twelve matches had been scheduled. Duntroon won against Sydney's Greater Public Schools on 9 June 1913 (12-nil) and played another five matches before an outbreak of smallpox in Sydney resulted in the cancellation of further matches. Further interruptions to the Rugby Union program occurred in 1914, again due to an outbreak of infectious disease—in this case, diphtheria.

The progress of Rugby Union during Duntroon's early years was, however, significantly influenced by other events beyond its control—most particularly the outbreak of the First World War in August 1914 which resulted in a rapid depletion of available players. The departure of the First Class saw the loss of half the Rugby Union team and by the end of the year all but two had gone to the war.

Yet, despite depleted numbers, Rugby Union continued to be played against visiting teams from Sydney Grammar, Newington College, The King's School, Sydney University, and, from 1916 a new competition began against the Royal Australian Naval College (RANC) at Jervis Bay. The first match

The Duntroon Rugby Union Team, 1915.
AWM P00151.002

was played at Jervis Bay in September with the host side winning 20-9. The following year, the match was played at Duntroon before a large crowd that included Brigadier General Parnell and staff, Mr W. W. Hill, the secretary of the NSW Rugby Union, prominent local identities and a contingent of ladies.

The match was refereed by Captain Broadbent and from the opening kick-off play was 'fast, open, and interesting.' The final result was a decided victory for Duntroon 47-nil. Similar results were recorded in 1918 (RMC 33-RANC nil) and 1919 (RMC 99-RANC nil). In 1920 it was decided that the competition would be more even if players were of a similar age. The result was, that Duntroon agreed to field a team drawn from the Third and Fourth classes, which meant that during the

1920s both sides recorded wins.

The inauguration, in 1917, of the Forsayth Shield competition gave an added impetus to the growth of Rugby Union at Duntroon. This annual event between representative teams from Sydney's Great Public Schools and the United Services (Royal Military College and Royal Australian Naval College) provided important opportunities for cadets to test their skills in a wide range of arenas.

The cessation of hostilities in November 1918, the aims of the 1919 Versailles Peace Treaty and the hope that the 'war to end war' had indeed secured a lasting peace was evidenced by a prevailing mood of anti-militaristic optimism. One effect of this was a decrease in defence budgets and a concomitant decrease in cadet numbers at Duntroon during the first half of the post-war decade.

Against a background of the depression of the early 1930s, the Royal Military College found itself temporarily relocated to Sydney's Victoria Barracks in 1931. Despite a lack of suitable sporting facilities at the Barracks, cadets soon found the availability of local teams meant increasing opportunities for competition. In the six years the College was in Sydney, Duntroon's First XV played around eighteen matches each season, establishing a reputation as an outstanding exponent of the game.

In 1931 and 1932 Duntroon participated in the competition for the Kentwell Cup, while from 1933 until its return to Canberra in 1937, the cadets distinguished themselves against public and government school teams, the Hawkesbury River Agricultural College and local army and navy teams. In its first year back in Canberra, the College won the Forsayth Shield and played a series of matches against visiting Rugby Union teams from Sydney. 1937 also saw the scheduling of a match between the visiting South African Springboks and the College—unfortunately cancelled due to an outbreak of German measles.

The following year Duntroon joined the Australian Capital Territory Rugby Union Competition and by 1939 was fielding a team in the senior grade and another in the lightweight grade—winning the competition by defeating Canberra's Eastern Suburbs 14-nil in the final. The outbreak of war in September 1939 did not unduly curtail sporting activities at Duntroon, which were regarded as a vital part of the overall training program and therefore continued essentially unchanged.

While it was more difficult to organize matches against external teams, cadets had many opportunities to participate in intra-collegiate matches, particularly against the officers' training wing. Though the traditional Forsayth Shield Rugby Union match was not held in 1940, it resumed in 1941 and continued throughout the war with Duntroon winning in 1941, 1942, 1943 and 1946. RMC also played other matches, for example defeating an Army XV in September 1942 in Sydney.

In 1945 the question of competing football codes (Australian Rules and Rugby Union) caused some controversy when a West Australian senator asked why cadets were not permitted to play Australian Rules. The official response from Duntroon not only argued that Rugby Union was the game played in the areas most cadets came from, but that much of the standing of the College was associated with the success of its Rugby Union teams—considered to be amongst the best in the nation.

Following the end of the war in 1945 cadet numbers began to increase and by 1950 Duntroon had three Rugby Union grounds and four teams. Rugby Union was going from strength to strength. Forsayth Shield matches continued—though not without controversy surrounding the ages and abilities of the cadets compared with the Sydney school boys.

Winning the Forsyth Cup in 1954 for the first time since 1949 Captain Staff Cadet Ian Mackay is carried off the field.

RMC Duntroon First XV, 1953.

The cadet teams of 1954-55 were considered among the best ever produced by the College. On 22 May 1954, the Duntroon team played the City Colts in the curtain raiser to the NSW-Fiji match at the Sydney Cricket Ground. Duntroon won 28-24 after being down 11-16 at half time, 'in a brilliant display of open football'. The RMC team comprised: I. B. Mackay (full-back and vice-Captain), J.A. McConaghy, P.N.D. White, J.G. Hughes, and R.G. Kennedy (three-quarters), D.V. Spicer (NZ), K.E. Newman (halves), M.M. van Gelder, J.E.E. Simson, K.J. McGhee, W.J. Meldrum (NZ), G.P. Carleton, W.T. Collins (NZ—Captain), B.W. Lake and J.D. McGuire (NZ), (forward). Mackay scored six goals—four penalties and two conversions) for 16 points in the match.

In 1955, Duntroon repeated the performance with a win over City Colts in the curtain raiser to the NSW-Queensland match in Sydney. In 1954 and 1955

Duntroon also defeated the Combined Greater Public Schools First XV side from Sydney for the Forsayth Cup, with scores of 26-5 and 28-11. Captured by the College, the trophy remains in Duntroon's hands in perpetuity. According to Ian Mackay, who captained the Duntroon side which won the final Forsayth Cup match, 'the headmasters of the GPS decided that they didn't want to play the Royal Military College anymore because they wanted to promote the GPS versus Combined High Schools game and so the game has never been played since, which is a great shame.'

While RMC had older and more mature players than their secondary school opponents, which at one time meant Duntroon was restricted to an under 21 side, Duntroon had actually lost the preceding four matches from 1949 to 1953. Overall, the Forsayth Cup was a great competition for Duntroon's First XV, while the Second XV played Hawkesbury River Agricultural College and the Third XV played Waverley College. 'It was a great spectacle and feature of rugby life from 1917—1955', said Mackay.

In the decades following the end of WWII, the rapid growth of Canberra impacted on the playing of Rugby Union in that there was a decline in the strength of the cadet teams in relation to that of the local teams. In 1963, RMC was defeated in the ACT grand final after winning the final the previous year; it never again won a first grade final in that competition. Although Duntroon continued to play in the ACT First Grade competition well into the 1980s, the end of the Forsayth Cup in 1955, the great wins over the City Colts in 1954-55 and the ACT premiership of 1962 closed a golden era of Rugby Union at Duntroon.

However, with the introduction of Service Teams from 1963 and triumphs for Army teams in the decade ahead, a new era was about to begin.

Second Half—
Australian Army
Rugby Union
1959-1972

Rugby Union remained as popular as ever in the Australian Army over 1959-1972. It was a period of great change. From a small force after the Korean War, maintained by national service to 1959, the Army grew rapidly through the 1960s as it undertook new overseas active service deployments as part of the Far East Strategic Reserve. Deployments included to Malaya during the 'Emergency', to Borneo during 'Konfrontasi' and then, from 1965, to South Vietnam. Even with the re-introduction of national service from 1964, the Army was stretched to its limits.

The Army XV, 1957.
Private Collection

However, wherever Australian units were deployed, Rugby Union matches were not far behind, whether at home or abroad; and the larger the Army became, the more Rugby Union was played.

One of the most significant overseas deployments for Australia since Korea began with the establishment of the Far East Land Forces (FARELF) from 1955 when Army personnel served with both HQ FARELF in Singapore or with 28th Commonwealth Infantry Brigade group based in Malacca, Malaya. The Australian forces were deployed to support operations in the Malayan 'Emergency' against Communist insurgents. The 'Emergency' was not declared over until 1960.

Based on an integrated British, Australian, New Zealand and Ghurkha brigade and supported by other arms and services detachments, it is no surprise that a strong Rugby Union culture soon developed in the brigade and in Singapore. In the early days of FARELF deployments, the Australian infantry battalion there at the time—2nd Battalion Royal Australian Regiment (RAR), 3 RAR and then 1 RAR—and other arms and service supporting units always provided a strong element to local teams. The large Australian contingent with HQ FARELF in Singapore also proved a mainstay of the success of that Headquarters team as well.

The competitions began at club level in both Singapore and Malaya, then inter-unit level, and then were fought out at HQ FARELF versus 28th Commonwealth

An Australian Army player gets away a clearing kick in the match against Fiji in the opening game of the Fijian tour of Australia, in Sydney 1961.

Brigade. Finally, it was the championship against other area champions in the Far East in a culminating Rugby Union finale in Hong Kong. Australians figured strongly in these competitions. Some, like Captain Ian Mackay, based at the Jungle Warfare School at Kota Tinggi, represented Malaya while others were chosen for joint service teams. In 1963, Mackay became the centre of an international dispute when both the Johore State Rugby Union (Malaya) and the Singapore Joint Services Rugby Union wanted to select Mackay for the Malaya Cup Competition. Mackay was a resident of Johore State but was administered by Singapore.

From 1963 to 1971 Far East Command was established with Singapore remaining as a major HQ.

The School of Military Engineering Rugby Union Team, 1963.
Private Collection

As an international command, the area contained FARELF, Australian Army Force and other naval and air assets. In turn this became the Australia, New Zealand and United Kingdom (ANZUK) Force. Australian Army personnel continued to be heavily involved in the continuing Rugby Union activities in the FARELF throughout the period. To give some idea of the number of the Rugby Union competitions being played, by the end of a three year posting in 1965, Major Ray Hilder, Royal Australian Engineers (RAE), of HQ FARELF had refereed 100 first grade matches across Malaysia.

Typical of the grand finals in the region was that played in 1968 by 8 RAR representing the Terandak, Malaysia, garrison, against a Royal Engineers side from Singapore—the winner to go to Hong Kong to play in the FARELF final. The captain of the 8 RAR side was Sergeant Les Fielding, a prominent Army, and later combined services player and coach. The British team included an Australian engineer on posting with the RE, Lieutenant Keith Alcock. 8 RAR lost the match, but had the satisfaction of having been the first team to beat the NZ XV in the Malaysia finals in six years to earn the right to go to Singapore for the FARELF final.

In another example of Australians on the 'wrong side', an Australian national serviceman, Corporal Max Mason of Australian Army HQ in Singapore, was the only Australian in the otherwise all British (and one Fijian) FARELF Crusaders team on a six day tour of Brunei units in 1968.

During 1962-1966 there was an Indonesia–Malaysia confrontation ('Konfrontasi') as Indonesia opposed, militarily and politically, the creation of Malaysia from the old Malaya, Borneo and Sarawak. Australian forces were engaged in Borneo, with other FARELF forces, countering armed incursions by Indonesia. Operations did not stop Rugby Union matches, nor did the 'terrain'. In July 1966, a match between 4 RAR soldiers was played near Bau in Sarawak, on a pitch which 'was a soccer field, grass knee high in places, in place of a touchline, a storm water drain—armed sentries guarded the field and players' rifles were close to hand.'

The Australian Army throughout these years also had a strong contingent based in Papua New Guinea, with engineers in particular, from Port Moresby to

Wewak. Again, a strong Rugby Union culture was well-established with Australian Army representatives in local and area teams, as well as in coaching and referee roles. One player of note who played in those local competitions was one Sapper Robert 'Danny' Kay, who had played in the Wallaby team tour of New Zealand in 1958, and would go on to further Rugby Union accolades in Australia. Kay later coached the Victorian Combined Services XV.

From 1965 Australian Army commitments to the growing conflict in South Vietnam began, growing progressively in size. By late 1972 when Australian forces began their withdrawal, a full Task Force was deployed. Again, Rugby Union wasn't far away. However, the operational tempo was far different to that of the FARELF/28th Commonwealth Brigade experience, preventing a high level of match organisation.

The 1968 grand final in South Vietnam was played out as an inter-corps, unit level competition for example—in this case, 17th Construction Squadron defeated 102nd Field Workshops. The oldest player for 17th Construction was the Officer Commanding, one Major Malcom van Gelder, an ex-Wallaby.

Like 'Weary' Dunlop in the Second World War, the war in Vietnam also saw another ex-Wallaby and doctor at work. Captain (Dr) John Bromley had played in the 1949 team against the visiting NZ Maoris and then went to NZ with the Wallabies later that year. He also played with the Wallabies in South Africa in 1953 but was injured in the first test. Bromley joined the Citizen Military Forces (CMF) in 1964 and volunteered for full-time service in South Vietnam; he returned to Australia in mid-1968.

The very first reference in *Army News* to a Rugby Union match in South Vietnam was in September 1965, played between 1 Logistics Support Company (LSC) and its Ordnance Detachment. Played in 90° in the shade temperatures at Bien Hoa, the reporter said 'Amazingly, no punches were thrown, and the match was played in the best of football code.' Perhaps not surprisingly, for the Ordnance Detachment team captain was none other than Captain Dave Spencer, who had played in inter-service and combined service Rugby Union in Australia.

A Rugby Union Team from Headquarters Australian Force Vietnam listen to Coach Major John McIntyre, 1969.
AWM LES/69/0675/VN

Teams from the larger Australian bases at Vung Tau and Nui Dat played throughout the conflict, while an Australian Army team called the 'Saigon Warriors' also played in Saigon at the former French sports club *Cercle Sportif*. Some of the 'front-line' troops had to wait until they returned to Australia to take on their rivals—for example, 5 RAR and 6 RAR, which had served together in 1966-1967, finally met on the Rugby Union field in Townsville in 1968, as part of 6 RAR's Long Tan day. 6 RAR won 15-6 (it was also premiers in the Townsville competition that year).

In Australia, meanwhile, the Army continued to evolve its structure and organisation to meet the changing peacetime and operational deployments. National Service, which had ended in 1959, began again in 1964. About 63,735 National Servicemen served in the military from 1964-1972. Of that number, 19,450 'Nashos' served in Vietnam, all with the Army. The rapid expansion of the Army during this period also meant that from 1964 in particular, there was an increase in all types of sport being played—this included a great increase in the number of fixtures in Rugby Union, especially in Northern and Eastern Commands (later 1st and 2nd Military Districts respectively).

Rugby Union was played across all Australian States and Territories however, not just in the two main Rugby Union States of Queensland and New South Wales. In the early years, Rugby Union saw a 'golden age' at Royal Military College (RMC) Duntroon. But other standout units engaged with Rugby Union included the Apprentices School at Balcombe and Officer Cadet School Portsea (although its team had a strong New Zealand representation) in Victoria, the Recruit Training Battalions in Wagga in NSW, the Special Air Service Regiment (SASR) in Western Australia and from April 1965 and for the next eight years, the Officer Training Unit Scheyville in NSW as well as the units stationed in the Enoggera Barracks in Queensland.

Matches firstly took place at inter-unit level. These were followed, from 1963, by inter-corps competitions and then inter-service competitions in each Command/Military District, sometimes under the umbrella of inter-service sports competitions. Occasionally, but not in every year, there were inter-service matches at a national level, but most inter-service matches were played out at the Command/Military District level—men were then selected directly for Australian Combined Services teams. In the meantime, many Army teams played in their State or regional competitions. In Victoria for example, Army fielded teams in the First, Third, Fourth, and Fifth grades of the Victorian competition, while in 1968, two Army Apprentices, A.C. Field (captain) and A. Vaughan, were chosen for the Southern States Junior RU team to tour NZ. There were numerous examples of Army representatives in interesting sides during the period—for example, in 1970 Lieutenant Wally Harris and Corporal Mick Strong were both chosen for the Singapore State side to tour Ceylon.

Unit teams fought for trophies such as the Commander's Shield in Phuoc Tuy province in South Vietnam and the Toomey Premiership Shield in Northern Command's inter-unit competition. The Forsayth Cup between RMC and Sydney teams was another well-known competition. Army players battled for the Ralph Sutton Cup in Singapore, the Kerin-Shergold Shield in PNG, the Perry-Uhlmann Trophy and the NSW Rugby Union Memorial Cup in Eastern Command. In a related Rugby Union trophy, the John Fraser Memorial Trophy was presented to the Southport School in Queensland by his father, John McInnes, Military Medal, after his son Lieutenant John Fraser, a national serviceman, who was killed in action in South Vietnam in March 1968. Fraser had played for the Combined Greater Public Schools XV, Gold Coast and Queensland Army Rugby Union teams.

The first representative combined services teams since 1954 also got underway in 1964, and thereafter an Australian Services Rugby Union began to develop the infrastructure to support ongoing combined services Rugby Union. Army was strongly represented in these combined services teams; a number of Army players were entered into Wallaby trials and three made it to the 1958 Wallaby side when it toured New Zealand—Charles 'Chilla' Wilson, Robert 'Danny' Kay, and Malcolm van Gelder.

Meanwhile Army players in Combined Services played for the WO2 'Dasher' Wheatley, Victoria Cross Memorial Trophy and the Lieutenant Des Ridley Memorial Trophy against Queensland. The Lieutenant Des Ridley Trophy, named after Ridley who was accidentally killed in late 1960, was an annual trophy competed for between Queensland Army and Brisbane teams between 1962 and 1964. From 1965, it was played for between Combined Services and Queensland. Ridley captained Northern Command Army XVs in 1959 and 1960 and Queensland in 1959. He also reached the finals of Olympic trials for boxing.

For every inter-service and combined service representative however, there were hundreds of officers, NCOs, diggers and trainees who continued to play their beloved Rugby Union without any expectation of becoming a Wallaby. Men such as Lance-Corporal Pat 'Dadda' Murphy of 2 RAR, who played his last match in 1965 after 25 years of playing Rugby Union, 14 of those in the Army, which he joined in 1951. 'LCpl Murphy estimates he has scored close to 2,000 points, playing five-eighth and full back.' Murphy said 'I'm definitely finished this time, but I hope to take up a whistle next season.' Players like Murphy and the many others like him were, and still are, the bedrock of Army Rugby Union.

A the School of Military Engineering Rugby Union Team, 1980.
Private Collection

Peace-keeping and Internationals 1985-2003

In the post-Vietnam War era and with the end of National Service, a reconfiguration of the Army posture took place. After a decade of strategic drift, with continental defence in vogue, the change was finally and clearly enunciated by the Dibb Review in 1985—'Defence of Australia' was formalised. One outcome from these changes was that for many years the Army essentially 'stayed at home'.

A rifle company remained deployed to Butterworth, a shadow of the former FARELF deployments, and an occasional sub-unit trained overseas with foreign forces. Compared to the previous decades in Malaya—now Malaysia—only one Rugby Union match was reported there between 1973-1984 in *Army News*. A team from B Company, 8/9 RAR defeated the local Tigers team in the Malaysian Rugby Union season, 21-3.

There were some small UN peace-keeping deployments until the tempo of peace-keeping operations began to change in the late 1980s leading to a major commitment to UN operations in Cambodia in 1992. One thing which didn't change was the continuous cycle, at least in Australia, of unit, inter-unit, inter-corps and inter-service Rugby Union matches. Combined service teams were by this time also a fixture of the Rugby Union scene, with Army dominating the Australian Services Rugby Union (ASRU) teams.

In a brilliant start to this new era, a young officer, Bob Brown, fresh out of Royal Military College (RMC) Duntroon's First XV, was selected for the Wallabies in 1975 as a full back. In his debut against England at the Sydney Cricket ground, Australia won 16-9 and Brown went on to play for Army and ASRU teams to 1985. Brown also played against England at Ballymore, the match again won by Australia. Brown would later become Chairman of ASRU (1999-2004) and a member of the ARU Board.

In Tasmania, Captain Bill Richards was selected for Tasmania and the 1975 ASRU team contained no less than 14 Army players. Meanwhile, veterans of the game such as Warrant Officer II Les Fielding at the Infantry Centre, continued to be engaged with Army Rugby Union as players or coaches.

In late 1975 the New Zealand Papakura Army team toured the east coast, with only 8/12 Medium Regiment unhappy with the outcome. The Under 19 South Australians played Victoria in 1976—two soldiers from 3rd Battalion Royal Australian Regiment (RAR) were in the South Australian team and no less than nine Army apprentices in Victoria's (Victoria won 20-8). This set the scene for decades to come—a busy round of Rugby Union fixtures, year in, year out.

By the late 1980s however, the operational tempo for the Army was to change once again with a ramp-up of United Nations (UN) peacekeeping deployments of various size and complexity in Rwanda, Somalia, the Balkans and the Middle East, culminating in Cambodia in 1992 and a decade later, in the Solomons and East Timor. The Army became stretched in ways it had not experienced since Vietnam. Rugby Union, along with other team contact sports, remained important to Army fitness. As the operational tempo moved up during the late 1980s and through to the end of the 20th Century, Rugby Union ramped up with it.

Views of fitness and how to achieve it became more sophisticated as well over this period. Touch rugby became very popular and a range of new sports were introduced for soldiers to pursue, from biathlons to cycling. Fitness for Army Rugby Union players has never been an issue, and this was recognised. For example, in 1979 the Wallabies were put through a gruelling training session by thirteen 2nd Military District Physical Training Instructors (PTIs) and in 1980 St. George went through the same torture at Holsworthy. For Army players, sport was only one of the fitness regimes available to help them become operationally ready, as many who played against them discovered after another hard match against Army.

In an inspirational Army Rugby Union story coming out of the Vietnam War, coach Lieutenant-Colonel Bill Rolfe was chosen to coach the 1979 and 1980 ASRU teams. In 1970, as a platoon commander in 2 RAR, Rolfe lost both legs below the knees in a mine explosion. He returned to duty four months later, and on his new legs, took to coaching the game he loved. There were plenty of matches to referee, for they were continuous across all levels of the Army, both in Australia and against overseas teams. Army's traditional enemy—Navy—remained the side to beat in the inter-service competitions (nationally and at military district and unit level). Over these years, the Royal Australian Air Force (RAAF) usually provided the warm-up match for the two dominant Rugby Union service teams. RAAF always fought hard but rarely prevailed. Typical were the inter-service matches of 1976—Army defeated by Navy 7-10, RAAF defeated by Army 17-0.

Navy defeated Army again in 1979, lost to Army in 1980, but lowered the boom on Army again in 1981, with the score 28-3. But in a glimmer of hope for Army's future, new strength was emerging. In that powerhouse of Army Rugby Union, the 2nd Military District (2 MD), six years of Navy dominance was broken in 1982 with a 20-3 win to Army. This saw the emergence of players such as Geoff Jones from 8/12 Medium Regiment who went on to play for Army and ASRU. But Navy defeated Army 22-10 in the national grand final of 1982, winning the Wing Commander John Caldwell Shield. Army replied in kind in 1983 and defeated the Navy team in a famous victory, its first against Navy since 1980.

The Army coach was former player Corporal Peter Ash, at that time with the School of Military Engineering (SME). Ash continued his coaching career with considerable success for Army and ASRU sides. In 1985 Ash won a Chief of Defence Force Commendation for his long and outstanding contribution to the sport of Rugby Union in the defence force, after playing between 1964 and 1978, and coaching from 1980. Ash went on to the Australian Defence Force Academy (ADFA) in retirement as its new coach.

Peter Ash.
Private Collection

In various 'internationals', an Enoggera Sappers XV were beaten 6-28 by a Royal New Zealand Engineers (RNZE) 2nd Field Squadron match in 1982, while in Germany that year a company from 5/7 RAR on exchange training played their host battalion, the Welch Fusiliers, downing them 28-20. One of the leaders of the infantry team was Lieutenant Martin Southward, who would figure prominently in Army and ASRU sides for years to come. Meanwhile in Malaysia, the infantry company on duty at Butterworth—in 1982 from 8/9 RAR—defeated the local Tigers to open the Malaysian Rugby Union season.

In 1999, the Rifle Company Butterworth from 25/49 Royal Queensland Regiment, was active in both the Kuala Lumpur Tens competition as well as the Kuala Lumpur Jonah Jones Rugby Sevens competition. In the normal three month tour for reservists, the Butterworth Barbarians also participated in the local rugby competitions.

In a joint exercise in Hawaii three years later, in 1985, a 6 RAR side overwhelmed its US hosts the 1/14 Infantry Battalion with a score of 28-0. In 1989, 6 RAR does it again, this time to the 7th Infantry Division (Light) with which it was exercising, winning 30-0. In 2002 6 RAR inflicted a huge defeat on the visiting French Marine Infantry Regiment team from New Caledonia, 67-3 but suffered a defeat in turn at the hands of a US combined services team at Enoggera, losing 7-17.

In 1987, a 2 MD team hosted by 8/12 Medium Regiment was cannonaded by a visiting Royal Horse Artillery Team, 28-0. The Land Warfare Centre managed to overcome a visiting Ohio State team 14-9 in the same year. Army usually, but not always, prevailed against American teams in Rugby Union. This was demonstrated once again in 2002 when a Townsville district Army team decimated a US Navy-Marine team from the transiting *USS Bonhomme Richard* with a one-sided 69-0.

The Royal Australian Electrical and Mechanical Engineers (RAEME) fielded a team in England for the EME World Championship in 1992. While it lost its tests there, it compensated with wins in matches against the Washington Combined Services (61-7) and Hawaiian Harlequins (37-0) on the way home. Meanwhile, the increasing tempo of operational deployments brought forward some interesting matches. *Army News* reported a match in Cambodia in 1993 between two Australian teams, and a New Zealand and British team, drawn from elements of UNTAC—with Australia going down to an undefeated New Zealand.

In 2000, a Rugby Sevens competition was arranged by the Dili Anzac Rugby Union Club in East Timor between Army, RAAF and NZ/Fiji teams. Towards the end of the Peace Monitoring Force (PMF) in Bouganville, Solomon Islands, in 2003, Army went under 18-42 to a NZ Army team supplemented with local Vanuatuans and Fijians.

The Army Rugby Union Team, 1985.
Private Collection

During this period to 2003, Army Rugby Union was not only alive and well for all of the traditional reasons but also because of the growing popularity of Rugby Union world-wide, enticing even American service teams to get more involved in the game at each opportunity. The variety and number of 'international' matches increased. While Army was not at war, new war challenges were approaching. In the meantime, home grown unit and district Rugby Union continued apace; with new developments in the formation of ADFA and women's Rugby Union teams yet to come. Even the RAAF seizes its moment to exact revenge on its long-time Army tormentors.

Wallabies and Wallaroos of the Post-the Second World War Era

Over the many years since the great AIF Rugby Union team of 1919, and the AIF team of 1941, there have been Wallabies who have served in the Army through to 1945. Names like 'Weary' Dunlop and Stanley Bissett from the the Second World War period often come to mind when Wallaby and Army are put together in the one sentence.

In a more recent conflict, Wallaby John Bromley (1949-53) served in Vietnam as a reservist on full-time duty. There have been other Wallabies too who served—and died—in the service of their country following the Second World War.

Others, like Pat B. Harvey, Ron M. Harvey, and Jim Williams, played Rugby Union while in the Army and went on later to become Wallabies, and in William's case, a Wallaby coach as well. This chapter, however, will focus on personnel who were chosen to be Wallabies while serving rather than on those Wallabies who were called up or volunteered to serve before or after their selection.

In the post-Second World War period there have been four Army representatives in Wallaby teams. They were Charles Roy 'Chilla'

Wilson, Malcolm van Gelder, Robert Cyril 'Danny' Kay and, and Robert Charles Brown. In this era, pioneering Army Rugby Union player Angelina Fairweather, selected for the first Wallaroo international, also 'gets a guernsey'.

Charles Roy ('Chilla') Wilson (1931–2016)

Chilla Wilson

Born in Brisbane, Wilson lived at Wacol and trained as a doctor, graduating from the University of Queensland in 1956 with MB and B.Sc. Later he worked at Mater Hospital in Brisbane. A brother, also a doctor, had joined the Army, and in December 1957 Wilson followed him by enlisting as a captain in the Royal Australian Army Medical Corps on a one year short service commission.

He was posted to the 1st Camp Hospital as a medical officer, attached to the 11th National Service Battalion. His commission was later extended by a further year and then again after service with 1st Field Regiment. Wilson left the Army in May 1959 and returned to medical practice, but stayed in the special reserve until 1976.

A flanker, Wilson joined the Wallaby tour of New Zealand in 1958. He had played Rugby Union continuously through Grammar School and University and like Malcolm van Gelder, was selected as much on the back of his University track record as anything else. His test debut was against New Zealand in Sydney in March 1957 and he played again in New Zealand as captain, culminating in the match against New Zealand in Auckland in September 1958.

Wilson went on to be manager of the Wallaby tours of France and Britain in 1976 and 1984 respectively. Mark Ella said of Wilson: 'I couldn't think of a better manager. I played for Australia for six years. Thank God I had Chilla Wilson for three of them...He was quiet, unobtrusive and didn't make a lot of noise. In fact, you wouldn't know Chilla was the manager until the time came for somebody to get up and say the right thing'.

Robert Cyril 'Danny' Kay (1935–2011)

Born in the Sydney suburb of Glebe, Kay enlisted in the Army as an apprentice in the 6th intake into Apprentice's School, Balcombe; his trade calling was as a carpenter and joiner. Kay served in the RAE, at first with the 21st Construction Squadron (1954).

He served in Papua New Guinea in 1962-1963 and later in operations in Sabah during 'Konfrontasi' in 1965-1966. He then served in Vietnam from March 1969 to March 1970 with the 17th Construction Squadron as a staff sergeant. Between 1971 and 1973 he again served in PNG. He was discharged as a WO1 in 1978.

A centre, he weighed just 76 kg when selected out of the blue for the 1958 tour of New Zealand, and was the first Victorian selected for Australia in 20 years. Jack Pollard wrote of Kay in *Australian Rugby*: 'He won his place in the 1958 tour of New Zealand with strong displays for Victoria in that he showed a grasp of the basic skills, proved a good link in the centres with his wingers and tackled heavily.'

Kay played as a centre for the second Test at Christchurch and noted New Zealand critic Terry McLean compared Kay's performance with a German band, for 'he popped up everywhere.' He again played in the centre in the 1958 tour for the second match against Wanganui—a match won 11-9 by Australia. Two matches later, against Nelson, Kay scored a try in a 20-11 win. Kay won selection for the second Test against New Zealand. The Wallabies caused an upset, winning 6-3. Unfortunately for Kay, an ankle injury sustained ruled him out of certain selection for the final Test against the All Blacks.

In 1959 the British Isles toured Australia, and Kay played against them for Victoria which was crushed 18-53. He was then selected for the second Test against the Lions; Australia lost 3-24. Kay once again lined up for a combined Victoria-South Australia team that played New Zealand in 1960.

From 1964, Kay played for the Footscray Club in Melbourne, scoring 12 tries in 29 matches in First Grade and four in Second Grade. Later Kay played for Randwick in Sydney.

Malcolm Montague van Gelder (1933-2008)

A member of the 1958 Wallabies team to New Zealand, back rower Malcolm van Gelder was born in Gunnedah, NSW, grew up in Warwick and entered RMC Duntroon in 1951. He graduated into RAE in 1955. He later served in Vietnam from February 1968 to February 1969 as the officer commanding the 17th Construction Squadron RAE. Leaving the Army after Vietnam service, van Gelder became a lawyer in Canberra, participating very actively in public life. A brother was a navy pilot who was killed in a plane crash in 1956.

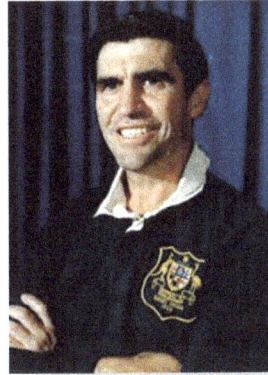

Malcolm van Gelder

While a proud military servant, it was in Rugby Union that van Gelder excelled outside his commitment to the Army. On the 1958 tour, van Gelder played matches against Southland and Manawatu on a 13-match trip. He scored a try on his Australian debut against Southland in Invercargill. After retiring from Rugby Union in 1969, he became a referee, officiating in 466 matches in the ACT. His last match as referee was as a 68-year-old in 2001 between a Seoul expats' team and a US Army side.

Although claimed by South Australian Rugby Union as one of theirs when van Gelder won Wallabies selection the season after playing with Adelaide University in 1956-57, he was by that time of selection in Canberra and playing with the Easts Club in the Canberra competition—so claims that he was the first ACT Wallaby and not South Australia's will always make for a good discussion among followers of Rugby Union history. Former team mates remember van Gelder as 'a marvellous, aggressive and attacking breakaway'. Aside from Rugby Union, van Gelder was the RMC middleweight boxing champion in 1952.

Robert 'Bob' Charles Brown (1953-)

Bob Brown was born in Parramatta, NSW and educated at Canberra Grammar School; he was selected for the ACT Schoolboys team in 1970. He entered RMC Duntroon in 1971 and graduated into Infantry Corps in 1974. While at Duntroon he played in Duntroon teams in two First Grade finals. Brown was also selected for NSW Country in 1973-74 and the ACT in 1973-1974. While in the ACT team, he played against Tonga in 1973, in the winning side against Queensland in 1974, and against the All Blacks in the same year. Selected for NSW in 1974, he toured the US, Canada and NZ.

Brown was selected for the Wallabies in 1975 while on his first posting to 5/7 RAR, when he played for Parramatta RU Club in the Sydney First Grade competition. Bob recalls that he played for Parramatta mainly through a friendship with dual international Ray Price, who represented the Wallabies in eight tests between 1974 and 1976. In the Wallabies, Brown played against England at the Sydney Cricket Ground (when he kicked a long range field goal) and at Ballymore in Brisbane in May 1975. He also played for NSW against England.

Injured in 1975, Brown chose to focus on his Army career—1975 was still the amateur era of the Wallabies and there was little incentive to leave the Army for full-time Rugby Union. However, he continued to play Army

Bob Brown

and Services Rugby Union, as a fullback, through 1985. He played for the Hunter Valley representative side while on posting to Singleton for example. He also gave back to Rugby Union, as Chairman of Services Rugby between 1999 and 2004, with a place on the Australian Rugby Union Board. Bob Brown is a career soldier, and currently serves in Canberra as a Brigadier.

Angelina Fairweather (1967-)

Angie Fairweather was born at Ballina in north east New South Wales in 1967. She was the grand-daughter of an Italian POW, captured at Bardia in the Second World War and interned in northern NSW—who after the war, collected his family and with others from Italy resettled back in Australia. Her parents were both Reservists and in 1986, Angie entered ADFA, graduating into the Army Intelligence Corps.

Playing touch rugby in and around Canberra while in officer training, Angie was deeply interested in Rugby Union but otherwise had no other opportunity to play the game. It was not until 1993, while on posting to the 1st Intelligence Company in Brisbane that Angie was able to become a foundation member of women's Rugby Union then being established there.

She began playing with Brisbane South at the old age—in Rugby Union terms—of 27. In 1994/1995 Angie was chosen for the first Wallaroos team to play New Zealand ('they absolutely slaughtered us—37-0'). Nonetheless, her Cap at No.15 in the Wallaroos 'hall of fame' will always sit proudly with her.

Army finally got underway with women's Rugby Union in 1995. Angie played for Army (1996) and ASRU (1997) teams and in the national titles competition in Darwin (1998) before age and motherhood got the better of her as a player—but she went on to manage both Army and ASRU teams in 1999. Angie Fairweather was one of the pioneers of women's Rugby Union at large and in particular was the first Army player chosen for the Wallaroos and its first international match.

Angie Fairweather

The Australian Army Rugby Union Women's Team, 2003.

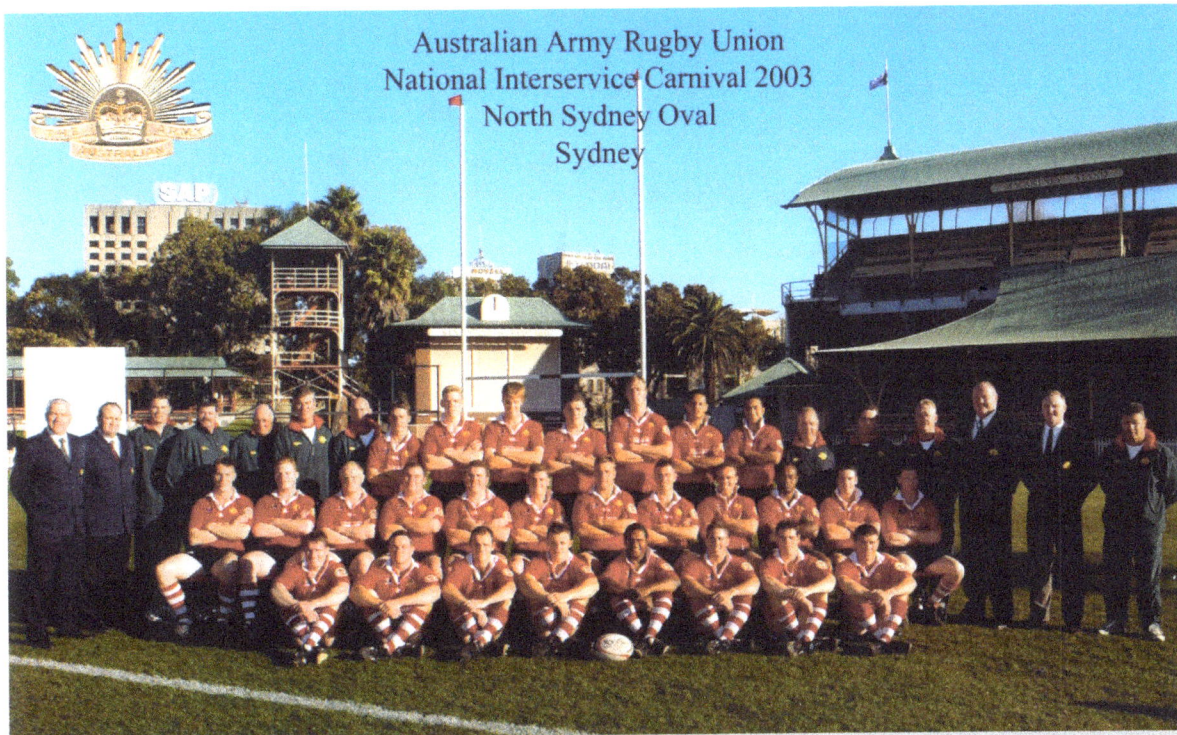

The Australian Army Rugby Union Men's Team, 2003.

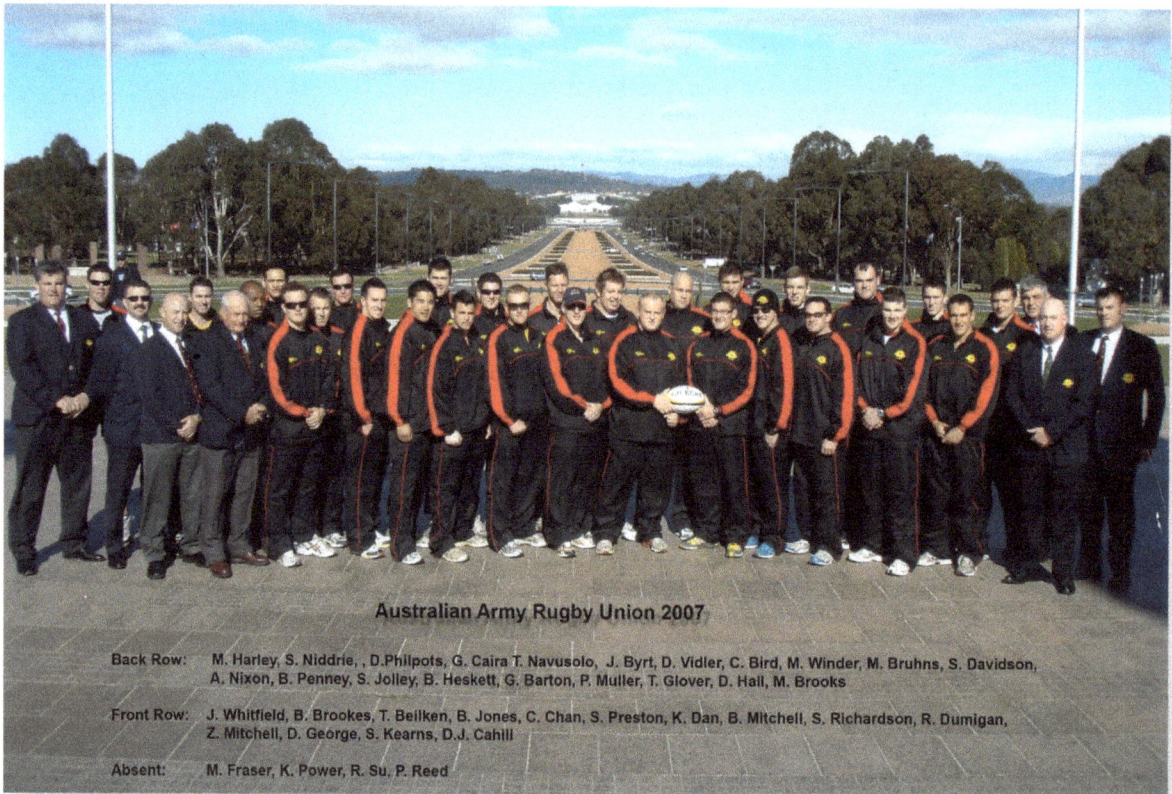

Australian Army Rugby Union 2007

Back Row: M. Harley, S. Niddrie, , D.Philpots, G. Caira T. Navusolo, J. Byrt, D. Vidler, C. Bird, M. Winder, M. Bruhns, S. Davidson, A. Nixon, B. Penney, S. Jolley, B. Heskett, G. Barton, P. Muller, T. Glover, D. Hall, M. Brooks

Front Row: J. Whitfield, B. Brookes, T. Beilken, B. Jones, C. Chan, S. Preston, K. Dan, B. Mitchell, S. Richardson, R. Dumigan, Z. Mitchell, D. George, S. Kearns, D.J. Cahill

Absent: M. Fraser, K. Power, R. Su, P. Reed

The Australian Army Rugby Union Men's Team, 2007.

Extra Time–Australian Army Rugby Union 1993-2010

In the period from 1993 to 2010, Army Rugby Union at home went from strength to strength. In 1993, the inaugural Kapooka Tens competition got underway. With 10 minute halves and 15 minute halves for the finals, it proved to be a popular initiative, created out of the 1st Recruit Training Battalion's (RTB) long-standing strength in Riverina Rugby Union. A decade later, it had dozens of Army unit teams playing in the competition from across the country. In 1996 the Royal Australian Electrical and Mechanical Engineers (RAEME) team defeated the British EME team in Hong Kong (27-7). Soon after, in New Zealand, it defeated the disbanded RNZEME, 46-5.

In 1999, in the inaugural Exchange Cup competition against the visiting Royal Engineers, the Royal Australian Engineers (RAE) team lost three times in succession: 14-24, 10-18, and 0-38. That year, a 'special' international tour was conducted when the Special Air Service Regiment (SASR) Rugby Union team toured the United Kingdom. The Australians defeated 22 SAS in a tight match 25-20, and then sank the Special Boat Squadron of the Royal Marines with a handy 43-12.

Visitors in 2001, the Royal Regiment of Fusiliers Rugby Union team were smashed by 'Old Faithful', the 3rd Battalion Royal Australian Regiment (RAR), with a 36-6 win. Then, in the RAE's 100th anniversary year of 2002, NZ Engineers came out on top over the RAE team, 25-0, in Sydney.

Inter-service Rugby Union finals continued the battle between Army and Navy, although the RAAF did strike back. In 1984 Army repeated its wins over Navy (8-6) and Air Force (23-7); but went under against Navy in 1985, 10-23. In 1986, the RAAF had a rare win over Army, 15-12, but Army still managed to down Navy 28-18. In 1987 and 1988, Army lost to Navy in the finals, won in 1989, only to be overcome in 1990. But then, in a remarkable winning streak,—apart from losses to Navy in 1999 (6-29) and 2005 (22-23)—Army dominated the series from then on. Army also dominated ASRU selections during this period. Army regularly provided at least half of the squad and often the majority in the teams. Army's traditional annual matches with the Randwick Club in Sydney, begun in 1978, also continued, with Army in general in the ascendancy.

Army travelled on several international tours or were hosts to international visitors over the period. In 1983, Army Rugby Union toured New Zealand—a first. It defeated the NZ 2nd Task Force Region 13-3 but lost by two points to the NZ Army, 14-16. One of the outstanding players was Lieutenant Dave Harper from 2/4 RAR, who later became a coach for unit teams and ASRU. In return, NZ Army visited in 1986. Army was beaten in the Sydney test 15-16.

In 1993, following a memorable defeat of the NZ Army under coach Bob Brookes, the AARU side travelled to Bangkok to take on the Royal Thai Army, along with the New Zealanders, at the invitation of the Thai Army Commander Major General Wimol. In the 12 day tour, the team was coached by Lieutenant-Colonel Larry Holme, assisted by Major Bob Brookes in his retirement year.

With the advent of the Australian Defence Force Academy (ADFA) in 1986, the first ever try by its new Rugby Union club in the senior Australian Capital Territory competition was made, with ADFA fielding teams across four grades. The emergence of ADFA as a Rugby Union force impacted on Royal Military College (RMC) Duntroon Rugby Union. Changes to the RMC courses also mean that reluctantly, in 1989, RMC conceded that it had to drop out of the ACT First Grade competition while retaining teams in the Second Division.

However, it continued its traditional Hatchet Trophy competition with the Australian National University, played for since 1965. In the eleven years that RMC played for the John Dent Cup in the First Grade competition, it won it seven times. Until 1963, RMC won 13 premierships and played in 18 grand finals. Since then, it only played in the 1972 and 1974 grand finals, losing both. Its Rugby Union heyday was over, but it left the First Grade scene with a proud record, with 120 cadets and staff alone representing the ACT since 1938.

There was another historical development in 1994. That year, Northern Territory-based Lance-Corporal Jodie Connolly, with HQ Northern Command, was selected to represent the Northern Territory in the National Women's Rugby Union Competition, the first soldier ever to do so. Not long after, new ground was broken again when Lance-Corporal Veronica ('Ronnie') May of RMC and Captain Angie Fairweather of the 1st Divisional Intelligence Company, were selected for the first Wallaroos team, playing in the inaugural women's match against NZ in North Sydney. Although the team lost 0-37, it is still history in the making for women Rugby Union players in the Army.

Army women and Army women teams went on to carve out their own history. In 1995, Connolly,

Angie Fairweather clearing from Fullback, 1994.

May and Fairweather were all selected for the second Wallaroos test in NZ, with lead-up matches against South Canterbury, Otago and South Land. In 1997, now Corporal Jody Collier of HQ 1st Division, was selected for the Wallaroos to play in the World Cup in Holland; and in 2001 Lieutenant Jen Egan of the 21st Construction Squadron also gained selection for the Wallaroos. Second rower Lieutenant Kate Porter was selected for the Wallaroos in 2006 and 2010, and prop Lieutenant Caroline Vakalahi also in 2010.

Australian Army Rugby Union international tours continued in the new century. In 2002 Army toured South Africa, where it defeated South Africa Defence teams in Pretoria (20-8) and Cape Town (33-19). The following year, British Army teams Pilgrims and Frogs visited on another 'special'. The Special Air Service Regiment defeated both but 4 RAR (Commando) could only manage a 10-all draw in its match against the Pilgrims.

An Army Rugby Asia tour in 2005 to Singapore, Beijing and Hong Kong was notable, despite a bad loss in the warm-up match against Randwick before departure, 17-52. But the team was bolstered by the send-off by Wallaby Drew Mitchell, who especially came to wish the team—and his two brothers in it—every success. In Singapore, the team won its match 40-5, and against China it won 47-15, but it fell to the Hong Kong Barbarians 26-36.

The British Army Rugby Union side toured Australia in 2007, smashing AARU in Sydney 36-0. A British Royal Engineers team then defeated the AARU Development Team 18-8, and the RAE team 32-15. Returning to France in 2008, the first time since the great 1919 AIF team played there, Army fought two hard matches against the French Army in Caen, winning 21-18, and against the French Combined Services at Vincennes, going down 16-27.

Army then travelled to Sennelager ('Camp on the Senne') near Paderborn in Germany to meet a representative British Army side, but again was defeated, 13-15. Back in Australia, and after a 17 year break, a New Zealand Army side visited and in a one-sided match defeated Army 32-3.

The decade ended on personal notes. The passing of ex-Corporal 'Blocka' Seruitukana was noted with sadness in 2008. With service in 1 RAR and with a deployment to Somalia, latterly with 25/49 RQR, 'Blocka' played for Army 30 times and for ASRU a further 12. His record was symbolic of the many Army Rugby Union veterans who went before him. The history of Army Rugby Union is full of men like Seruitukana, hard playing, a good friend on and off the field. Not all got to play for Army representative sides, but played on in unit and local Rugby Union competitions regardless. Men like front rower Sergeant Ken Gibb, formerly with 3 RAR and 6 RAR, of the Special Forces Training Centre at Singleton,

The AARU Men's Team versus the French Army, 2008.

who in 2008 managed to complete 200 matches in the Singleton Lions, Newcastle and Hunter Valley 'C' Grade competition. "I keep returning for the camaraderie", he told *Army News*, in a perfect summary of Army Rugby Union since its earliest days.

The AARU Men's Team 2008 Tour of Europe.

The AARU Women's Team at the Australian Services Rugby Competition, 2008.

The AARU Men's Team versus the British Army, 2008.

The AARU Women's Team versus the Combined RANRU and RAAFRU Women's Team, 2010.

Interview with Ian Mackay–Australian Army Rugby Union 1952-1969

I wonder if you could tell me a little bit of biographical detail—where you were born, where you lived and your family background.

I was born in Summer Hill in Sydney in 1934 and went to school at a marvellous Demonstration School in Haberfield—very high standard and then on to Sydney Grammar, with a minor hiccup of going to Fort Street, which was a selective school. Sydney Grammar was a great experience. I was in the cadets. I had some motivation as a pretty reasonable sportsman—much more than an academic.

And that obviously links to eventually having a military career?

Well it was a pretty complex situation somehow tied up with rugby. I had been injured quite badly—I had broken my knee cap in one of the early games of the season in 1951. We had a very successful Sydney Grammar team in 1950 in which I was a 15 year old full back and got selected for GPS and was obviously showing some promise. However, I broke a knee cap in one of the early games in 1951 when I repeated my Leaving because I was pretty young and that went undiagnosed for six months.

I got back on my feet and later in the year, was selected as wicket-keeper for the GPS First XI on the Sydney Cricket Ground against a New South Wales team, captained by Ritchie Benaud. I managed to finally get a diagnosis and my knee cap was operated on in January 1952. I arrived at Duntroon pretty late in first term of that year.

My parents were very supportive. My father had played for New South Wales in 1926, there was no Australia in rugby terms in those days—but he played against a New Zealand side and he was an understudy to the great fullback, Alex Ross in Australian Rugby early history.

What did your father do professionally?

He was a businessman and worked for an Argentinean firm.

That would have been unusual in those days, I would have thought.

Yes. It was a successful world-wide firm called Bunge, principally in the grain trade. He was very interested in my career. My grandfather had been a very keen fosterer of my father's career and had kept a very good scrapbook. At the behest of the Australian Rugby Union, I gave them a lot of that history and they copied much of my material, which they didn't have in their archives.

What was your motivation to join the Army?

My motivation was partly tied up with the fact that I was told that I couldn't play football for 12 months, because of the knee injury. I was actually at Sydney University commencing Engineering and I had been selected for Duntroon. I decided, almost on an impulse that if I couldn't play football, I would go off to the military. My uncle, Lt Roy Mackay had been killed on the Kokoda Track on Armistice Day in 1942—almost at the 11th hour of the 11th day.

Who did he serve with?

He served with the 2/31st Battalion AIF soon after he was commissioned in the field. He was a platoon commander in D Company. Most of his platoon was wiped out with him– his very good buddy was his platoon Sergeant Jimmy Gordon VC, who had been with Roy in the Middle East.

I would have been about 6 years of age when he went off to war but I did remember him quite strongly. He was a factor in my motivation for the Army. He was the youngest of ten of whom eight children survived. My father was the oldest. They had big families in those days. There is not a great deal of military tradition in the family but he was certainly an inspiration to me and so I went to Duntroon in 1952 and arrived at the Royal Military College.

Does that mean you were a late intake—because of your knee?

Well, yes. I had actually been selected to be first selected in the group so they took me at this late time and I was ushered down to see the Regimental Medical Officer, Major Nimmo, who was related to General Nimmo (World War 1). On the first day there, Major Nimmo and then Captain Norrie (later General Norrie) put me through a bit of a medical interview. Captain Norrie was coach of the RMC Duntroon team and the doctor cleared me fit to play the next week in the opening match of Rugby commencing in Wagga after the war. So in 1952, within a week of arriving in Duntroon, I was off playing fullback for the Duntroon XV.

And this was how long after the surgery?

Probably three to four months. I was operated on in the January and this was early May. Within a few days of arriving at the College I found myself playing in a very important match against a Combined Riverina team, which got Rugby back on its feet in the Wagga district after the War. And I played against a future competitor for State and Wallaby selection as a fullback in my later representative career, Maurie Graham. So that was pretty interesting. My papers had been marked not to play rugby for 12 months but the authorities didn't seem to notice that. They needed a full back.

So obviously you went through Duntroon playing Rugby?

Yes. We had a good four years and the highlight of the season each year was to play the Combined GPS First XV, which was a great day in the rugby calendar of Sydney and Australia in those days. Many of the future Wallabies came particularly out of the GPS team—not so much out of the Duntroon team—but it was a great rivalry. It was called the Forsayth Shield, presented by the then Governor-General in 1917. I have some photos of the Shield because we won it in the last two years of my captaincy, which was 1954 and 1955 and so the Shield remains in perpetuity with the Royal Military College. In fact, I found it in the Quartermaster's Store at the Royal Military College a few years ago when I was trying to present it to the NSW or the Australian Rugby Union, because it is a magnificent piece of rugby history.

The game was called off in 1956, after we had convincingly won the two games in 1954 and 55, with scores of 26-5 and 28-11, from memory. The headmasters of the GPS decided that they didn't want to play the Royal Military College anymore because they wanted to promote the GPS versus Combined High Schools game and so the game has never been played since, which is a great shame. When I later became coach of the Duntroon team, I went to see Sir Leslie Herron, who was the President of the NSW Rugby Union and Chief Justice of NSW and asked him to see if we could get the game on again. He explained to me that the reason that the game was deferred was that for some subliminal political reasons, they were trying to stop soccer getting into the High Schools. So that is a bit of a view of the rugby politics. It didn't do any good anyway. It was like King Canute trying to hold back the tide, so it was disappointing that a great fixture was abandoned for very short-sighted reasons.

I would also assume that you at RMC would have actually been older—more mature—than the secondary school boys.

Yes, we were and at one stage Duntroon was restricted to an under 21 side but Duntroon had lost the preceding four games from 1949 to 1953. I played in two of them—52 and 53—and GPS soundly thrashed us. It is just that we had a very good team in 1954 and 1955 and then most of us graduated and there was nobody over 21, I am sure. We really had a pool of players to play from of about 20 competent people, whereas the GPS schools had so many more. It was a magnificent fixture and it is a shame that it passed out of the game.

And that is part of the history, of course, isn't it?

Yes, it is part of the history and of the GPS schools and Australian rugby because some of the people who were playing for GPS played for Australia the following year. So the story that the little school boys weren't big enough or tough enough was not really valid, because they had so many to select from and they were great teams. Anyway, it was marvellous to have the 40 or 50 years of the traditional game, which was sometimes played as a curtain raiser to Test matches but often it was just the main game—the GPS Firsts played Duntroon, the Seconds played Hawkesbury Agricultural College and the 3rds played Waverley College. It was a great spectacle and feature of rugby life from 1917—1955.W

When you graduated from Duntroon, where were you posted?

I was posted to the 4th Battalion of the Royal Australian Regiment in Sydney and I went straight into the Randwick First Grade side, which was a marvellous team with many internationals. I was stationed at Ingleburn and so I drove the 96 km round trip for practice on the Tuesday and Thursday, when I could, to play with Randwick and it was a magnificent side.

Did many of the Army people play with Randwick or was it just you?

No, it was really an association of my father's. Most of the Army people in that area would have played for Parramatta. I played actually four seasons across six years for Randwick and ended up captaining them in the latter part of my final year in Sydney rugby before departing for Malaya. I did play representative football for the Australian Barbarians in their initial match and against Fiji and the All Blacks in the period 1957 through to 1961.

So you weren't actually playing with the Army rugby team?

Of course I played for inter-service sides—I captained the successful 1957 Army side in which we beat the Air Force 17-9 and we drew with the Navy 9 all. There is photo of me being presented with the McCabe Cup by the Governor of New South Wales, General Sir Eric Woodward, and I am fairly certain that it is actually the Stan McCabe Cup, which must have had a pretty interesting history. I don't have details of it but Stan McCabe was, of course, a famous cricketer who must have been also involved in rugby. So I am delighted that I received the McCabe Cup on behalf of the team, because I was a great admirer of Stan McCabe as a very courageous cricketer in the Bradman era.

Now from Ingleburn and Sydney, I think you said in your CV that you served in Malaya.

Well 1957 was a pretty momentous year because that year the Wallabies were planning a 7 month tour around the world including Europe, the UK of course, and America and Canada.

You wouldn't have been granted leave to go on that.

The press was touting fairly solidly that I was likely to be selected. At this stage I was under consideration for the Wallabies for this marvellous trip around the world. Unbeknown to me, Lt General Berryman had been approached by the Rugby Union and instead of going to Malaya with a lot of my contemporaries in that year I was held back. The reason I was held back was to go with the 1957 Wallabies. This was all done without my knowledge but I was actually told by an Australian selector three days before the team was announced that I was chosen for the Wallaby tour covering full back and three quarter positions and would be on full pay attached to the Brigade of Guards. A subsequent letter from the Australian Rugby Union confirmed that I should prepare for inclusion in the team.

Instead of that marvellous trip, I came down with a severe bout of hepatitis, which was a very new disease to Australia, the night before the Australia v The Rest game. That was the final Wallaby selection trial and it is one of the great regrets of my life. I spent three months in Concord Repatriation Hospital, instead of being on the high seas with all those marvellous footballers touring the world and playing top rugby. Three months later I staggered out of hospital with orders to do nothing terribly strenuous for the next 12 months.

So I was posted to the Special Air Service instead. Ironically, I went around to Perth on a ship-these were very different times. I went to my posting in Perth on a ten day voyage on a ship the SS *Strathmore* which was the one the Wallabies had gone to the UK on three months earlier. The crew could not wait to tell me about the marvellous time the fellows had. I arrived at Swanbourne military camp but on the first afternoon, my platoon was sent on a 20 mile route march on the sand, with me having been in hospital for three months. The temperature was above 100 degrees Fahrenheit and the platoon virtually carried me back to camp I suspect. I managed to keep up the appearance of leadership but it was a pretty fierce entry into the military world.

What was your rank at that time?

I was a Lieutenant and 1957-58 were marvellous years with the SAS and some rugby also featured. The disappointment of not being away with the Wallabies was partly eaten up by the fact that I ended up being appointed captain of the West Australian rugby team, which was a forerunner of the Western Force today in the Super 15 competition. We went to Melbourne and I ended up being the captain coach because the coach, who was a very senior international referee and manager with the ANZ Bank, Jack Maclean, couldn't get leave.

So I became captain/coach at the age of 22 with a group of fairly wild Western Australians and we actually won the Southern States carnival. I don't think West Australia had won many games ever before in the tournament and we had a magnificent series. There are some great photos of the Cup being presented and there is one me actually drinking out the Cup, standing on the platform in Kalgoorlie en route back to Perth.

So that is 1958 and SAS days. After leaving SAS on promotion, I became Adjutant of the 11/44th Battalion (City of Perth Regiment) for a period of time and then had some time in Brisbane during which I played for the GPS Club. There was an Army team in Brisbane but I had just arrived on a 6 month stint and I played with the GPS team.

What time is this?

This is 1959 and had a pretty successful season but managed to smash myself up in a trial game before the British Isles versus Queensland match. I played for Brisbane against Toowoomba in the final trial. I had broken my wrist in the first 60 seconds of the game, which I only discovered late on the Sunday evening after the match, when the euphoria and the alcohol wore off. I had scored 32 points in the game and was selected for Queensland for the Tuesday night match against the British Lions but I ended up in plaster on Monday morning at the Brisbane Hospital.

You wouldn't have played for the rest of the time, I wouldn't think.

No, my arm was in plaster and I don't think I returned to the game that season. But in late 1959, I was back in Sydney and posted to Holsworthy Camp. I was appointed Adjutant of the 2nd Battalion, The Royal Australian Regiment at and we were slotted to go to Malaya in 1961. Lieutenant Colonel Adrian Smith (Joe) Mann, DSO, MC was CO and then later we had a Pentropic Battalion organisation. We were the 2 RAR Battle Group under Colonel Keith Coleman—an ex-Armoured Corps officer. In September 1961, Lieutenant Colonel Stretton, later General Stretton of Darwin fame became the CO and we took the battalion to Malaya.

There was a lot of rugby in Malaya in 1961 to 63. Commonwealth Forces South was the team in the Malaya Cup Competition, so it is very relevant. I was only in the Battalion for six months in Malacca and was posted to the British Army Jungle Warfare School in Johore State. I can give you two and a half years of rugby in Malaya in two or three paragraphs that I think is relevant because it showed that while Confrontation was on with Indonesia, there was still rugby played and very good rugby, actually.

And how long were you in Malaya for?

Nearly three years and Malaysia was formed towards the end of that time in late 1963. And that would have been the peak of my rugby career in Australia and, of course, I was in the jungle instead. But we did play a lot of rugby. I can summarise it in a couple of paragraphs if you would like. I think it is relevant to be included because it is associated with the Army and Commonwealth forces and shows that the Australians, New Zealanders and the Brits all played together. I think that is interesting for the history of Army rugby.

In Malaya, the 2nd Battalion moved into the new Teredak Barracks out of Malacca—it was a big, new 11 million pounds sterling barracks built by the British and handed to Malaysia a few years later. As Adjutant of the 2nd Battalion, we had a very good rugby team and played in the local competition. There was a wider group called Commonwealth Forces South and I played for them as full back and captain for a couple of years—from 1961 to 1962.

It was a very good competition with some top grade British and New Zealand players including the odd All Black and English trialist. We had a very successful rugby team in that Malacca Barracks. I was posted from Adjutant of 2nd

Battalion and became instructor at the Jungle Warfare School in Johore at Kota Tinggi on the east coast of Malaya. It proved a very interesting international jungle school, probably the best jungle school in the world.

It is important to fit rugby in because I captained the Johore team in that inter-regional/ interstate competition. One of my highlights, unfortunately, was to be captain of the Johore team that beat Commonwealth Forces South—my old team. We beat them 9-6 in a magnificent game on the Johore Padang and my digger mates, with whom I had played previously, reckoned the victory with the odd bare-footed Malay or Indian winger beating the Commonwealth Forces South team was quite an achievement.

I also was travelling to Vietnam quite regularly. As an instructor, we had Vietnamese officers and NCOs and I travelled to Vietnam on a number of occasions between 1961 and 1963 and on one occasion I actually played rugby against the Royal Navy for the French Club Cercle Sportif—a marvellous club in Saigon. Somehow or other, I was on a weekend break In Saigon and played and actually scored a couple of tries against the Royal Navy XV.

When the game was over, the Admiral presented the cup to the Sportif and he said to the captain, 'Mackay, you travelled up with us from Malaya, why didn't you play for us?' and I answered, 'Well, you didn't ask me to play for the Navy and these people offered me a game when I was in a bar in Saigon.' That didn't please the Admiral but we had a marvellous game. It just showed the spirit even at the height of the war—there were still some interesting sport and fun to be had.

I returned to Australia at the beginning of 1964 but actually was in a Combined Services Singapore team, which toured West Australia in 1963 and it was a very successful tour. It took us two days to get from Singapore via Penang and Cocos Island to Perth and we had about a 10 day tour of West Australia. It was great to be back there because, of course, I had captained West Australia before and it was a very successful tour. I also played for All Malaya against Thailand. At that stage there was a number of service people in that game in 1963. Before Malaysia was formed in September or October, 1963—it was called Malaya. So it was actually an All Malaya side. That was a great tour with some very fine football. It was the cream of the services and civilians in that Malayan competition. Back to Australia in 1964; posted as an instructor and company commander at the Royal Military College and obviously, appointed to coach the very important RMC First XV.

I have already mentioned that I tried to get the GPS Duntroon game on again with Sir Leslie as soon as I took up the job in February 1964 but to no avail. Duntroon were pre-eminent in the local competition in Canberra and we had a successful time over those 3 years of coaching. In 1964 I played for the first time for the Australian Services as captain with Colin Kahn as the coach, and we had a very good tour of the States. We were beaten—we only had one win, I think, but the tour was quite successful. I think we were playing the best in the land. As a subsequent footnote to that—eight years later, I coached an Australian Services team that was undefeated on that similar tour and we only had one first grade player in that team. That was 1972 but I have jumped out of context there in terms of time.

I fractured my skull in my last game in 1964, playing for Australia Services against Victoria and ironically the fellow who jumped over me when I forced the ball behind out goal line was an Army player, who should have been playing for us but he was playing for Victoria and his boot just caught my head so that was the end of my official Army career. There is a photograph of me in rugby gear, when we played one game in Vietnam in 1966-67 with the 6th Battalion. I was Company Commander, B Company 6 RAR and we played A Company and there is a photograph somewhere of me with the steel helmet, which we played for. It was a terrible climate and it was a crusty hideous ground but it was a great morale booster for the troops to see a game of rugby being played and particularly having Company Commanders involved with them.

Well that sounds good actually. I understand that you still meet with your mates from the Army Rugby Union team?

Yes, we do meet but somewhere in my notes, it was talking about Duntroon classmates—50 something years on. Our numbers are dwindling but we do meet every six weeks or so at the RSL in Kirribilli and we reminisce fondly but our numbers are shrinking. We are now down to about a handful.

How many of those were rugby players with you?

One of them certainly—and one just died recently—a New Zealander. But there are two of them who were rugby players with me in those teams that I talked about at Duntroon. So it is a great relationship and the camaraderie is still there and very strong.

There are just another couple of snippets. I was a keen referee and in 1969 I was appointed to referee the Australian Services game versus Queensland at Ballymore. I appeared in the programme as Col I Mackay. I was a full colonel at that stage but some of the diggers who were from Enoggera Barracks—when they saw me run out on the field as a referee; I got a lot of encouragement throughout the game. They were calling out 'Come on Col come on Col.' I thought it was a bit strange—the conservatism of the Army listing me as Col.

But it was a thrill to referee at that level. Queensland won that game very convincingly and it was the Des Ridley Trophy, who was a very fine Army rugby player, who had died at a very young age. So the Des Ridley trophy still exists for competition between Australian Services Rugby Union and Queensland. Probably one of the biggest thrills of my life was to see the 1972 ASRU team, which I coached, defeat Queensland at Ballymore. They were a top Queensland side, which had just returned from an undefeated tour of New Zealand and had at least seven Wallabies in it and our boys won 27-25 on the bell.

The Queensland victory was really a magnificent effort which capped the tour where they beat Combined Australian Universities, a Combined Sydney XV, the ACT and the Darling Downs. Finally an undefeated tour and in that side there was only one first grade rugby player and we beat the best in the land. That was a lovely climax to my rugby career and there was a photo in the Courier Mail of me and also Butch Baker the captain, being hoisted the next day and I noticed that my hair was wet. And I said, 'why were my clothes wet?' and they said that it was raining for the last 15 minutes and I didn't even notice the rain. It was so exciting and it was such a magnificent effort by these young fellows, some of whom are still playing rugby in West Australia.

There are two of that team, now in their mid-60s and one of them is with the SAS and the other is a captain of industry and those two fellows (Bruce Hughes and Geoff Stooke) with a combined age of 125 + are still playing for an Associates 4th/5th grade team in the rugby union competition in West Australia.

That is amazing. It obviously gets people in. Thank you, Ian.

The AARU Men's Team versus the RANRU Men's Team.

Interview with Arthur Fittock – Australian Army Rugby Union 1958-1974

Arthur, can you give me a little bit of information—biographical information please about yourself—when you were born and where and a bit about family and education.

I was born in 1939 in Bundaberg and my father moved the family to Toowoomba in 1941. My Dad had been a First World War veteran and joined up in 1941 in the Second AIF. Later, he opened his practice [solicitor] in Toowoomba and that is where I grew up. It was a strong rugby league town.

My rugby career began in 1951 as an under 6 stone 6 rugby league player and then I played for the next couple of years in the under 7 stone 7's for the East State School and played for Toowoomba in 1953. From that I was selected to play for Queensland. We toured New South Wales playing NSW in Sydney, Wollongong and Newcastle.

In 1954 I went to The Southport School as a boarder and stayed there until 1957. There I played Rugby Union, firstly in Under 15s then seconds, and was in the first 15 in 1956 and 57. I was captain in 1957 but was injured early in the season.

During 1957 I visited Duntroon with a group of school cadets and I met Peter White, who was a final year member—a cadet at Duntroon. He was a member of Duntroon's First XV and we watched them play on Saturday afternoon. It was good fun and an enjoyable outing. Afterwards he said to me, "Why don't you come down here next year. It has better food than boarding school, you get paid—and the Army is interesting." So I duly applied and went to Duntroon in 1958 and I guess that changed the rest of my life.

So when did you play in the Army rugby union?

At Duntroon, I played in the first 15 all four years—1958 to 1961. I was captain in 1961 and was awarded an Honour Cap which I still display proudly. Duntroon played in the ACT competition and played in the finals each year I was there. In 1960 and 1961 we were Premiers. While there in 1959, I was selected to play for the ACT and forget against whom. I was selected again in 1961 but because of duty, was unable to play.

After graduating in 1961, I moved to Melbourne in 1962 to finish off my Civil Engineering studies. There I played for an Army team in the VRU A Grade competition. The team had little support beyond the players and rarely trained together. Our home ground was Broadmeadows and players came from a variety of units and locations. We players organised the uniforms, balls and linesmen. After our home games we hosted the opponents in the Canteen at Broadmeadows—and that was always good fun. Our social life through rugby was probably better than our performances!

So it was an informal organisation?

Yes, it was. Well there was a team and I had a jersey and we played in the comp and all that business. Without any high level support, we muddled through. Really it was a bunch of junior officers with the odd soldier playing in the Victorian comp (VRU A Grade). I was selected to play for Victoria in that year. Victoria played a team from Japan and the Junior All Blacks in 1962. I also played in the Wallaby trials in Sydney but was really not fit at the time—my fault.

Colonel Bill Henderson came into Victoria before the next season and took control of Army rugby. Hence in 1963 he got rugby organised in the normal Army way. He decided that the A Grade team would be based on OCS Portsea with invitation players coming from around the metropolitan area. Portsea had a coach, Captain John Maguire from New Zealand, and in 1963 and 1964, we did quite well, making the finals in each year. The 1962 experience was overtaken by keen support from the senior officers and a team which played together but was unable to train together. Two PTIs from AAS (Jim Hope and Jim Husband), Ken Leckenby from Pucka [Puckapunyal] and good strong fit cadets were supported by a group of young officers studying in Melbourne. The team was happy, focussed on Saturdays and home games were at Portsea. After the games, our social life was a significant highpoint!!

In 1963, with the Victorian team I played at the Australian Carnival in Sydney, which is also part of the selection process for the Wallabies. The carnival involved teams from all states and the Queensland team included players I knew from school days. Sadly I was not good enough then to make the Wallabies. 1963 also saw the resurrection of ASRU and this team toured by train, the Eastern States. My Army team mates included Charlie Barnett, Billy

Jaego, Reg Sutton, Colin Hickton, Gordon Anderson, Neil Condon, Blue Hodgkinson, Graham Walker, Duncan Spencer and Jack Byrnes. Our results were not good—but it was a good start for ADF rugby.

For the first few months of 1964 I moved to Sydney for a course and I played the first half of the season with Parramatta A Grade as the inside centre. Parramatta had become home for Army players based in the Liverpool Holsworthy area and looked after us well. This was an interesting time. Parramatta trained on Monday night and Thursday night at the Parramatta oval. At SME, my team trained on Tuesday and played in the Wednesday Army competition. So I trained Monday, Tuesday, play Wednesday with the School of Military Engineering, trained Wednesday night, played Saturday and had a rest day on Sunday. What else was I meant to be doing??

The Army competition was Sydney wide and quite a lot of travel was involved. Fortunately on the same course was a great NZ mate, David Maloney who propped for Parra, SME and later ASRU. We had played together at Duntroon and here we were together again.

By sometime in June I was back in Melbourne—re-joined the Army team, the VRU team and ASRU. ASRU Army mates that year included Ian Mackay, Jim Herron, David Wilkins, Duncan Spencer, Butch Baker, Ron Sherman, John Essex—Clark (who had migrated from Rhodesia), Dave Shergold, Jack Byrnes, Eric Williams, Peter Ash, Tom O'Brien, Bill Jaego, Ted Stevenson, Ross Hutchinson and Dave Maloney.

And at this stage were you married with a family?

No, in 1964 I was getting married—it was late in the year—December. My wife Margie was a true blue Victorian, loved Aussie Rules, supported Melbourne and had never seen rugby until she met me.

By then you had completed your Degree, I presume, at Melbourne University?

No, I was at RMIT. I was having great difficulty doing this course because of football.

I would imagine trying to fit in the study would be difficult.

And, of course, in Southern Command in Melbourne, there was a big inter-service competition between the Navy, Army and Air Force. So I was doing a lot of sport and not too much study.

Yes, I can appreciate that.

In 1964 I said to the Army that I was getting married in December. Consequently I would not play football in 1965 and will finish my studies. I eventually did.

You mean that marriage was a steadying influence?

Yes. The result was I went to Borneo at the end of 1965 and left my wife of one year at home with a new baby.

And how long were you in Borneo for?

> I was in Borneo for 6 months and came back in mid-1966. As soon as I got back we were up in Shoalwater Bay—for three months and after six months in Borneo, there was no footy that year.

And you didn't play rugby, obviously, while you were in Borneo?

> No, we were all over the place up there. There wasn't any real sport in Borneo. At the end of 1966, I was sent up to Brisbane to 18th Field Squadron. In 1967 I played with the GPS Old Boys' Rugby Union Club in A Grade. I had a very successful year with them and I was picked as one of the best 5 players in Queensland.

> I was a captain, running a unit of 270 blokes. Of course we had a rugby team too. At the time Bobby Templeton, the Queensland coach asked me to join the Queensland squad. I attended training a few times but soon realised with my unit, Club and family commitments, I just did not have time. He sat me on the reserve bench for Queensland when we were playing New South Wales—but I did not get on the field and hence failed to play at senior level for my home state.

That was a disappointment, I would imagine.

> Well it wasn't really. I just didn't have time. I was busy. I had a pregnant wife—we were expecting our second child, I was loving the unit, I was playing football for the Army.

What rank would you have been at that stage?

> I was a Captain.

A lot of administration, I suppose, and responsibility.

> Well it was busy. Vietnam was on and all of the regular people were lining up to go to Vietnam and be part of the AFV.

And did you succeed in that—in the end.

> Yes, eventually. Before hand in 1967, the Army had a terrific team in Northern Command. We won the inter-service. Next the Qld Combined Services Team played Queensland. Some of my team mates from GPS were playing for Queensland and so we had a great battle with each other. I remember there was great joy at the time on both sides.

> John Stephenson was up there too for the game—he was running ASRU then and asked if I was available. I told him that I was too busy. 1967 season was interrupted by a deployment to Shoalwater Bay yet I managed to play in the Queensland Grand Final for my Club GPS. After five weeks in Shoalwater Bay, an interview with the General running the exercise after the *Courier Mail* said I would be home for the match, and a night train trip from Rocky to Brisbane, I was not really in the best of form for a final. And we lost! My fault probably.

After the season closed, we moved to Townsville with 18 Field Squadron. Our second child was born in Brisbane thus 1967 had been an adventurous year. By early 1968, I knew I was off to Vietnam in May. Townsville time flashed by as all the preparations took place and by May, I moved Margie and our two daughters back to Melbourne.

Unbelievably I ended up working for John Stephenson. In the dry season he had me organise a Rugby Union team to play in Vietnam. We did that—and played right into the finals I think ...

Who did you play against?

We played against other Army units. There was only a very short season and it was in the winter up there.

Where were you posted?

I was at Headquarters of the Australian Logistic Support Group. Colonel John Stephenson was the Commander and I was a Captain. We got beaten in the grand final of that comp that John Stephenson set up by 17 Construction Squadron. So here I was playing against some of my old mates. Corporal Danny Kaye (RIP) played for the Wallabies and he and I played with each other and against each other in Victoria over the years. That was interesting. In 1969 I came home and went back to 21 Construction Squadron at Puckapunyal.

My unit had teams in the local competitions and I occasionally played. In 1970, approval was given for me to organise a team from Puckapunyal to play in the VRU 3rd Grade competition. With Ron Sherman, David Gillette and Dave Hannell, a team was organised and put in training. We put lights on the oval at Pucka [Puckapunyal] and began the routine once the season started of playing in Melbourne one week and the next at home. It was most successful and kept going through to 1971.

We had a good team winning the 3rd grade very easily in 1970. And we did that again in 1971. As usual our families were great supporters—washing socks and jerseys, looking after the kids at the games, travelling to and fro. Amazing stuff really, and our team mates just fitted in very well. I think occasionally we would put on the field as many as five players who had played in ASRU and First Grade matches in Canberra, Melbourne, Sydney and Brisbane. Sometimes getting players free of duties was challenging but we seemed to get through most of the difficult stuff.

And did you retire from Rugby at that stage?

No, I didn't. In 1972, I went to Staff College down at Fort Queenscliff and there was no football that year.

In 1973, I was posted to the School of Military Engineering in Liverpool and I didn't play football at all in 1973. I was getting pretty used to not being able to play. But in 1974, the CO/CI, who was retiring said, 'Look I want you to play football again this year. I think we have a fair go of getting into the finals.' Thus in the Army competition in Holsworthy, I played again in 1974. We made it through to the grand final and we were beaten by 5/7 RAR. That was a sad occasion. I probably played so badly that it was getting near time to hang up my boots. In the end I went off to America and was there until 1976.

I came home in the beginning of 1977 to be the commanding officer of 1 Field Engineer Regiment and, of course, I played with my unit there—albeit in the seconds.

What would you be—late 30's by then?

I was 38 or 39. I was still fit and strong. I stopped playing after a young gunner ran me down and jumped on me from behind... a couple of weeks later the MO said I could go on playing but it might lead to permanent damage to my neck—it was time!

I was thinking that—what about injuries? You probably became a bit concerned about getting injured.

Well, when I was playing my really best football, I guess I used to tear my hamstring from time to time. That was a serious injury really and, of course, I had never had the patience to wait for it to fix properly. I would play again and then it would go again. So I think when I had the best chance of representing the country, I had this problem with my hamstring. Anyway that is life and that goes on. I was injured by a Japanese guy—he sent me to hospital for a few weeks.

Was that in Australia?

I was playing for Victoria and I guess I had bad ankles at various times but really, you know, apart from the normal rough and tumble of the game, I was pretty lucky as I don't have any problems with my hips, knees or ankles. The few teeth that went missing have never been a real inconvenience.

I was thinking that. Do you suffer from these old rugby injuries now?

I suffer from sore hips from time to time from being bashed around a bit.

What are the highlights that you would see, of your playing career?

Well, I think captaining the teams is always something I enjoyed. I liked getting blokes together. You know, I played with some terrific players over the years and I had some good coaches when I was young—from the time in Toowoomba in 1953 onwards. And at Southport we had not bad coaches. Duntroon was good. The Army and Defence tried hard to make it all work. So the people I played rugby with all through—were very close associates, not necessarily best mates. We shared something special and hopefully won modestly and lost gracefully. If I ever see them, and I recognise who they are, there is no doubt we are best mates. I think that is a major highlight.

An interlude of interest is the fact that in 1964 when playing at SME, we persuaded the US Army Exchange Officer to play with us. He had played gridiron for West Point. He learned some of our game very well indeed. Then move forward to 1975, and I am the Aussie Exchange Officer at their Engineer School and he is back at West Point as a colonel. He ran the West Point rugby program! He invites us up to West Point—we see the grid iron game on Saturday and on Sunday, he wants me to talk to the West Point rugby teams. When I asked how many—he said 14! Hard to believe but there they were. I talked to a few!

And the camaraderie of the game?

Yes, you know it is wonderful all over the world. And of course, the social side of rugby was always very attractive too. While we did some dumb things, it was really quite orderly in many ways and it was nice for the girls too. My wife, who grew up in Victoria and went to Lauriston School, fitted in well all over the world. She has seen a lot of rugby games and fields.

She didn't know much about rugby union?

She knew nothing about the Army and about Army people, let alone rugby. Anyway, she still barracks for Melbourne in Aussie rules but she has become a really staunch Union person. She knows all the Wallabies and is very keen on the Brumbies from our years in Canberra, even though I have converted to the Reds since we moved back to my home state.

When you say the social side, did you have functions and that sort of thing or just the camaraderie generally?

My experience is that most after game activities were informal—organised localities and come if you want. Rep games had formal functions. Regardless of type, the socialisation between teams and officials was fun filled and pleasant. The tough confrontations were left on the field—and the joy of the game left most in great spirits.

Now can you also tell me please, how many of the Army Rugby Union teams' coaches can you remember in detail?

Yes, well at Duntroon I had Colin Khan (Kahn) and Brigadier Geoff Leary—Col was a captain then and Leary was Lieutenant Colonel. They were terrific. Kahn also coached the Australian Services Rugby Union. John McGuire, a New Zealand captain at Portsea when we were doing well in Victoria—he was just an excellent coach. He had been a great player and, in fact, he probably could have kept playing because he was only a captain at the time, but he had some injury that prevented him from doing that.

In Sydney, we would often be looking around for who was going to coach and often it would be one of the players. At one stage Danny Kaye coached one of the teams that I was playing with when I was SME. In my unit, we would just appoint anybody—someone who knew about it—to be the coach and he would tell us all what to do. So that was really nice. John Stephenson was a terrific coach and he had a strong interest in the game right up until he passed on.

We had really good blokes in the rugby circles. Ian Gilmore was a referee in Sydney and he was a great mate of Roger Vanderfield. Ian is still alive—only just—but in Brisbane. In Duntroon in the final year, we went up to Sydney to play soldiers from 1 Division. The soldiers were looking forward to putting these officer cadets in their place. Our half back was punched in the open in the nose and rather than retaliating, swore loudly at the aggressor. Immediately, the whistle went, I was summoned and the half back was warned that any more bad language would result in a send-off. Ah justice!! We still talk about it!

This is actually on the field, I presume.

Yes, on the field. This was a nice way of saying there are a number of standards and you have to put up with that. Today, Army football is a long way from me but Margie and I remain absolute devotees of the game as do our children, their spouses and our grandchildren.

So you obviously still keep in touch.

Yes—and my old playing mates are still in my network.

So really quite a strong network?

Yes, it sort of goes on and on and on. I am interested in the game still.

Can you remember any personal stories about incidents that happened?

Well, I think one of the nicest stories I have is about Reg Sutton, who was five eight in my first three years at Duntroon. Not long after he left Duntroon he was playing for Parramatta. In 1961 I think, he was selected for the Wallabies to go on tour in New Zealand. Rather than accept the selection, he told the ARU that he was going to get married. We all told him that he was mad but anyway—that is what he did.

Hopefully he has never regretted it?

Well he never regretted it. He was awarded a Military Cross in Vietnam but sadly, he had a terrible time with his health.

You would know each other pretty well, I would imagine?

Sure and most players have really close contacts with those who shared on field experiences. One of my class mates who replaced Reg Sutton as 5/8 in 1961 recently died in New Zealand. My last conversation with him involved telling him how happy we were with him as the key distributor—he responded with the thought that he was lucky to play with such good blokes. The other thing about Army rugby is when you are playing with the soldiers, ranks disappear on the field. So we are all one...

So there is a good relationship—a camaraderie developed?

Yes, there is a good relationship.

Another story involves Tony Larnach—Jones at Duntroon—his Dad was very involved with the game in Sydney. In 1961, two of us—Jack Burns, he was another classmate of mine and was our front rower—and I stayed with old man Larnach—Jones. We were there to play Hawkesbury on the Saturday—before Wallaby Fiji test. We won as I recall. Next morning, Larns' old man offered to take Jack and me to the Bondi Diggers. This was a new experience. It was a big club on the Esplanade at Bondi. Some 150 odd men were there and Tony's Dad wanted to introduce us to the gathering.

How did it come over?

He told these people about these boys from Duntroon and that they were up here playing rugby and that they are the future of our Army. They won yesterday and, of course, in Bondi Diggers, it went down very well indeed.

We got much applause about it all. It was very humbling really but also it was a nice thing to do.

The Army moves folk around a lot and of course that provides benchmarks. Generally we can track experiences by locations, dates and activities. When Reg Sutton was at Duntroon as a lieutenant colonel, he coached the First XV from which he came. He would ask me from time to time to join him. We would stand together on the sidelines. Sometimes I would be invited to give the boys some rallying words. What I remember most about that—I used to always say to them, 'What will happen today is if you run out on that field and do your very best and win, as time goes by, you will forget about it but if you run out on that field and don't play as well as you can and lose, you will never forget about it.

Was that accurate?

I certainly think so—and I found that throughout my rugby career that the games I lost when I figured that I could have done better were the games that always stayed in my mind. They still do!

They were often thought of as that lost opportunity or not focusing on the moment. Nonetheless I have seen some great contributors to rugby come through the Army—not too many Wallabies—van Gelder, Kaye, and Brown—and today in professional football it is hard to see the Army featuring. Still it is good to see Peter Cosgrove on the ARU Board.

A pleasant memory relates to my attending a Ballymore game in 1989—the Wallabies were playing. An early curtain raiser featured John Eales in a Brothers underage team. The famous Paul McLean (Wallabies in the 1970s) approached me as I was walking to my seat. He pointed out a tall young player coming from the field, and he said to me, 'See that tall kid coming off the field over there, his name is John Eales. He is going to be one of the best rugby players this country has ever seen.' And how true that proved to be.

As the ASRU representative to the ARU Council in 1982 to 1984, I was thrilled to see the Wallabies prepare for the undefeated five nations tour. Allan Jones was the coach and the captain was Andrew Slack. At a farewell function that ASRU put on for them at Rugby House in Crane Place in Sydney, there were a number of lovely speeches. Finally it was the coach's turn—Alan Jones said 'I want to show you how well we are prepared. We are training very hard as you would expect but we are also doing better than that. We had some choir practice and I want you to hear the Wallabies sing. The Wallabies went up to the end of the room and sang the National Anthem. What an impact that had—amazing, and since then at our footy games, you hear everyone sing the National Anthem with gusto.

It really was good?

Yes. It remains a nice little story and it showed how thorough Jones was and no wonder he has gone on to great success. And the results of the tour were exceptional—undefeated.

And Arthur you still go and watch the Wallabies, but you don't see any Army Rugby Union games?

No, I haven't. Look, I really just watch the Super 15s and the Wallabies. The only other games that I go to are my games. I have two grandsons presently playing—one is 13 and the other is 11 and they have both got broken left arms at the moment.

Are they from separate families or the same families?

The same family has three boys, my other grandkids are girls. I have told the boys that they are going to have to improve their tackling techniques. By the time I watch them and watch the Super 15s—that is about all I do now.

And I was going to ask you—did you ever actually have any trophies?

Trophies lose some relevance with time—I do retain my Honour cap from Duntroon, the pewter from Queensland for the best five players of 1967, an ASRU trophy from the 1964 tour and photos of some of the teams. Premiership Trophies go on and on with the relevant union. The first trophy I ever won came when I was playing for Queensland as a 14 year old and I won a pair of football boots. It was for best and fairest in the Queensland team.

Is there anything else that you can remember to tell me?

No– I haven't been very generous with my comments on other players but I guess that is life. I have played with lots of terrific players over the time. Some on my side, some against.

Arthur, thank you very much.

Interview with Angelina Fairweather – Wallaroo

Can you give me a little bit of detail about yourself please, for instance your date of birth and where you were born, a bit about your education and when you joined the Army.

I was born on the 2nd of June, 1967 on the far north coast of New South Wales in a town called Ballina. My mother's family had pioneered that area a couple of generations previously.

All of them lived around a little town called Woodburn, which is about 30 kilometres south of Ballina. So I grew up there. My father was Italian. His father had been taken as a prisoner of war during World War II and brought out for internment here in Australia. At the conclusion of World War II he went back to Italy to get his wife and three eldest children and in the time that he was in Italy, another two children were born, including my father. Then they came out to Australia and another two children were born out here.

So it was quite a large family?

Yes, 7 in all and they went and set up on the north coast of New South Wales on a cane farm because that is where he had been sent to work as a prisoner-of-war. A lot of the Italian prisoners ...

You are talking about World War II, aren't you?

Yes. He was captured in the battle of Bardia in north Libya and my Mum's family, as I said, were pioneers of the area and her father was an apiarist and had bees everywhere over the place. My parents married quite young—they were both 17.

Where were you educated?

I grew up in Woodburn and went to a very small school—the central school which went right from kindergarten through to year 10. I did all of my schooling there. After that you had to go to one of the bigger country towns for senior school. So I went to Ballina and finished years 11 and 12 there.

Did you go straight into the Army?

Yes, I joined the Army straight out of school. So the idea, I guess was—my father had been in the Army reserves and my mother had joined the Army Reserve at one stage—the 41st Battalion in Lismore.

So you had a little bit of a family tradition there?

I wouldn't say that. I certainly didn't feel it at the time. I liked the idea. I had done Girl Guides and Brownies. I was a fairly disciplined child and I liked the regimentation, I guess and we didn't have a lot of money and I didn't like the idea of having to put any financial pressures on my parents and the Defence Academy was opening up—I cannot recall how I ever heard about it—but I applied for that in year 12. I went through the selection process and was part of the first intake to start there in 1986.

Well, that was an interesting beginning.

Yes, for sure.

So how many years was that then—two years?

Three years—and you do your officer training at the time you are doing your degree at the Defence Academy. But as an Army officer in training, you then finish your final year over at the Royal Military College at Duntroon.

And is that when you decided that you would join the Rugby Union team? I assume you play a variety of sports.

Yes, I had played a lot of sport in high school and I played some representative sports in softball and soccer. I knew nothing about Rugby Union basically until I joined the Army because the far north coast is pretty much a Rugby League heartland and that was all that was ever played. I remember our school team once played a game of Rugby Union just for fun against the high school. That was about it. I probably saw it flicking over on TV a couple of times but I had no real interest or knowledge or background in it at all. When you join the Army, it is quite big. The Defence Academy had a big Rugby Club. My boyfriend, at the time, was playing a lot so I used to travel around with the boys and I just loved it—I loved watching it and I loved the culture of it.

What was special about the culture? Can you explain that a bit please?

It was just the tradition of Rugby and there it is tough while you are out on the field but afterwards you go and have drinks with the opposition and all is forgiven and you have a good time.

Yes, the camaraderie. And you as a woman, when did you start? Surely one of the traditions at that time—you wouldn't have ...

Women's Rugby wasn't under consideration or on the radar but what did start in the late '80s was touch football.

At the Defence Academy?

No, not the Defence Academy but in the ACT and New South Wales and there were competitions outside the College and I used to go and play in a mixed team with some of the staff and students at the Defence Academy and that is when I really found that I really loved running the ball and working together as a team. I did quite well at touch football as well. I really liked that. I always wished I could play Rugby but it just wasn't on the cards. I played Rugby League as a little girl but when I got to the age of 13, they made me stop.

So when did you play Rugby Union with the Army?

What happened was—in 1993, I was driving up on exercise to Shoalwater Bay and I heard a radio interview with a lady who was trying to start women's rugby in Brisbane. I was just so excited and she was talking about how they were going to have the national title the following year and then they were going to select a team to play against New Zealand. I was just beside myself, "that's it, I am going to play for the Wallaroos. I want to be part of this first team". So as soon as I got back to Brisbane, I got involved with her and helped her establish women's rugby in Brisbane.

So you were stationed in Brisbane at the time?

Yes.

And who were you serving with?

I was with the 1st Intelligence Company.

So therefore you could actually play civilian rugby as well—I mean, you weren't necessarily doing shifts or that sort of thing?

You had to apply for permission to play any civilian sport and when you got selected to go higher, you had to apply for permission to go away and do that as well.

So you started playing for Brisbane?

We started up a competition with about 8 teams which were based on the 8 premiership clubs here and we started off with a 10 a side competition in the pre-season and then we went to a full 15 a side with under 19 rules because the girls had not grown up with rugby and it was quite dangerous to be pushing in scrums and that sort of thing. It is a bit different and coming into a sport like that as an adult and not growing up with it—the contacts and all that sort of thing. We just took to it like ducks to water.

So you had a group of similarly enthusiastic females?

Yes, a lot of girls had followed their boyfriends around and had an interest and skills in playing sport. We also had a lot of girls who were quite skilled at touch football and wanted to take it to the next level. In fact, a lot of the girls who came into it from that way knew nothing about Rugby Union, knew nothing about the traditions of the game, knew nothing about the Australian Wallaby teams. You would mention a player and they would go 'Who?' It was a bit frustrating with some of them.

Did you actually get involved with playing it for the Army—the Australian Army Rugby team—at that stage? When did that occur?

That started in 1996. We had two years when we played for civilian clubs in 1994 and 1995 and then I was selected to play for Australia in both of those years. Then in 1996, they decided to hold a women's competition with the Army versus Navy versus Air Force. I didn't play then because I had become pregnant at the time. It was in Sydney.

They must have had enough support for a Navy and an Air Force team as well.

Yes, I think so. I wasn't really involved in it in that first year. When the next year came around in 1997, I played for Army in that year and then we selected an Australian Services Rugby Union (ASRU) team to go and compete in the Women's National Titles. We sent a team down there to Adelaide.

And what do you remember—any highlights of your playing career that you can remember?

There was not a lot of opportunity to play for Army. There were no selections as far as I recall. Most of us had been playing for civilian clubs. We got together for about two days of preparation and training because you put your name in. I can't even recall how the team was selected and you turned up to the Army versus Navy and Air Force and you played each of the other two teams and they selected the ASRU team from that.

So you wouldn't have had the same sort of continuity and involvement that the men would have.

No and not the amount of development. It may be different now. I have just been to see the ASRU girls play at the national titles here and they are a lot more professional and sophisticated so I guess there is a lot more development now....

It must be pleasing, after 15 years, to see how it has developed.

Yes.

And you wouldn't have had trophies, I presume or that sort of thing, that you were playing for?

I don't recall. It didn't seem important.

So it was really just a pleasurable game that you could get involved with and there wasn't, for instance, a long tradition of obviously ...

It was important—the red Army jersey—it is a striking uniform and when you pull it on, you do feel a sense of representing the Army. I remember a male friend of mine—I think he had played for Army many years ago, he was telling me all about it. So there was this sense of tradition which all the girls felt very keenly—I gave him my jersey and he was absolutely rapt.

Do you regret that now?

No, because back then we didn't have our own jerseys. They gave us the men's ones. They were oversized and tatty. It wasn't a great look but at least you were wearing Army Red...

You felt identified—yes.

It was far too big for me. It was difficult for me to play in.

So you didn't play in any international matches—they would have purely been national ones?

That's right. Army didn't play against anyone else except Navy and Air Force.

And you played in Adelaide—and where else?

That was an Australian Services Competition and at the end of that, the Army, Navy, Air Force competition—they picked an ASRU. The first year was '97 when we played in Adelaide and in 1998 we played in Darwin in the national titles.

ASRU?

That is picked from Army, Navy and Air Force.

What were the ASRU colours?

The uniform is a red, dark blue, light blue with a white striped jersey.

Do you still have one left?

I have both of them.

So you kept some memorabilia?

Yes.

Any trophies or records or programs or souvenirs like that? Have you managed to collect any of those?

No.

Just your jerseys. And how long—you only played it for 2 years?

Well in 1999 I got pregnant again with my second child and by that stage I was in my thirties.

I guess it would be a bit rough for young mums.

Yes, I decided at that stage to just switch to Rugby League. I wanted to try and be a dual international so I played in 1999 for a rugby league club here in Brisbane. Then I fell pregnant half way through the year so gave it away. By that stage my body was telling me to give it away—like you play for 80 minutes and you would be sore for three days. It just wasn't worth it.

Not as you are getting older too, I guess.

I was quite old when I started playing (27).

What about—you never got involved with organising or any administrative position?

I did go back after that and became manager of the Army team and then the ASRU team.

Any outstanding players you can remember or any particular games that were significant?

I just remember in that second year—the Army versus Navy and Air Force in Brisbane in 1998 and the Army team for that year—we were only away for about a week but we were very close. It was a great feeling. We won the competition that year. We had a great proportion of Army girls in the ASRU team as well.

There was a young player that year from the Defence Academy called Jen Egan, she was the hooker and I think it was quite an achievement because I had been back to ADFA a few years earlier on and I wanted to donate my Wallaroo jersey to ADFA to make a display in the sportsman's Lounge and she came up to me and said that she was inspired by that and that has what had gotten her into rugby. And she actually went on to be selected to play for Australia as well. So she played as a Wallaroo.

Can you tell me a bit about when you were involved with the Wallaroos?

That was back in 1994/95. We formed these clubs here in Brisbane—the national titles were held in Newcastle that first year. We thought we were pioneering women's rugby in the world and we were the first people to play women's rugby.

Well you would have been, wouldn't you?

Only in Australia—well not even really in Australia because we got down to these national titles—we took our club side down. There were about six of the Brisbane club sides ended up going down from Brisbane and we got down there and there were teams from New Zealand and the ACT and New South Wales and places like that and they had been playing amongst themselves for a couple of years.

The New Zealand women's team had even gone to Europe and contested against England and the USA so we were really way behind the eight ball. We got down there and we did quite well—my club side Brisbane South. I think we came 3rd or 4th that year and we had six or seven girls in the Australian team. So we were very happy. We were winning our club competition up here as well. That year they arranged for the New Zealand girls to come over here to Australia and toured around the country and played an invitation New South Wales and ACT side and then they played Australia in Sydney. That was the first taste of playing for Australia. It was just a one off test and they absolutely slaughtered us—34-0.

So nowadays, I am thinking of the parallels between the two—there would be quite a few of the Army Rugby Union team that might, in fact, be selected for the Wallaroos.

That is possible. What they do these days—they have got them in two separate pools. So the top pool has teams from the strong areas like Queensland, New South Wales, New South Wales country and the ACT. Then they have got a second pool from the weaker areas—West Australia, South Australia, Victoria and ASRU. So it is more than likely that they would take the majority of the Wallaroos from that top pool but it is still quite possible, and I know some ASRU girls have been selected recently.

If you go to the Australian Rugby Website and you have a look at the Wallaroos page, there is a list on there of all the Wallaroos and their captain and their numbers and you will see that I am listed as number 15. It has got the state of origin there and I think that I would be written down as Queensland because that is where I was first selected. But if you go down the list, you will see a few girls there from ASRU—over the years.

Can you remember anything more you would like to tell me about it? Apart from Jen, who you mentioned before, it there anyone else who might have been significant in the team or people you know of still who are playing.

I remember when I first got selected and this was before the Army, Navy, Air Force thing, there was Colonel Bob Brown, at the time, I think he is Brigadier now.

I think someone else has mentioned too that he was involved with them.

I got a hell of a lot of support from the Defence Force and the Army, particularly when I was first selected for the Wallaroos and I got congratulations and they also offered to cover all my costs and pay me extra money. They were very, very supportive and giving me the time to go away with the Australian team.

How much extra time did it take? How much time did you have to take off for these sorts of events?

I had quite a heavy training regimen in the months leading up to it and also we would go away for training camps beforehand—probably up to two weeks.

And would you have several of those a year?

This was just in the lead up to the test matches. We toured New Zealand so we were away for two weeks. I didn't need approval that year because my husband had been posted to Vanuatu and we were actually spending time there—I am pretty sure I was living over there or about to go and live over there with him.

So you got time off to come back over here and train.

I wasn't working at all. So I would come back and play here. I was playing wherever I could get a game.–

This is before your babies arrived?

Yes. We went to England and I played over there and I actually played for the local ex-pat team in Vanuatu. I was playing as much rugby as I could find and then I would come back here and play. I got selected for the Australian team again.

It must have been quite a challenge in the tropics.

Yes, it is, especially when the ground slopes and is covered in coral.

And what did you play in—boots, I presume.

We played normal rugby but it was just a little bit difficult. We played against a lot of the local teams—the soldiers and the police and things like that.

Did you find that you had a lot of injuries?

No, I was pretty lucky. As I said, I played for an ex-pat team so it was full of Poms, Australians and Kiwis and they were quite protective of me as a female in a men's game.

Angie, you must have had a very non-traditional involvement. How do you feel about it from this distance?

Looking back on it now, it does strike as quite an amazing time. There were a lot of firsts in my life that really didn't strike me at the time. Now that I look back on it, I was in the first intake into the Defence Academy and part of the first team in Brisbane and the Wallaroos team, the first Army team, and first ASRU team. So I guess it is significant.

Do you recall having any difficulties as female players?

I do recall in the early days of women's rugby the coaches had to stand outside the dressing rooms waiting for the girls to change before they could go and speak with them whereas normally they would just be in there with the male players.

It would have been quite a bit of a juggle. Thank you, Angie.

Interview with Dr Charles Wilson –Wallaby

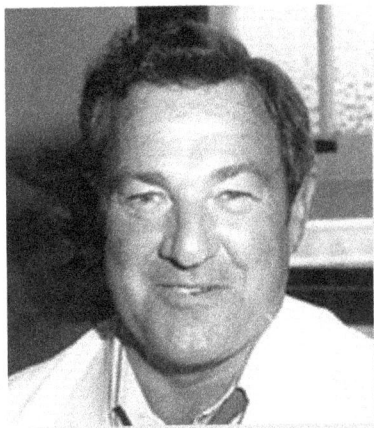

Charles, could you give me a little bit of detail about yourself, your education, where you were born and educated, and what you were doing when you joined the Army.

I went to Marist Brothers College Ashgrove initially, as my education and then went to the Brisbane Grammar School for five years. I graduated then and commenced doing a course in medicine, which was a six-year course at the university. I took seven years, I won't tell you why—not thinking properly. So at this stage I was playing rugby with the Queensland University side. We had a very strong side. I played for them for about five years in the A Grade. We won the premiership five times in a row, so we were very strong.

Then from the medical point of view, I did my traineeship at the Mater Misericordiae Hospital in Brisbane, and finished the course and at that stage I was contemplating going overseas, so I had to do something, so as my brother had—[he was] an orthopaedic surgeon, he was a captain in the Army for a couple of years preceding me, and he talked me into joining the Army, because they then were incorporating starting a Rugby Union side to compete in the Brisbane competition.

Now that suggests you joined the Army just to play rugby. Is that correct?

No, it wasn't really correct. I couldn't—I had finished my term at the hospital and my brother advised me if we were going to go overseas and get a higher qualification, as was the thing to do then, that he encouraged me to join the Army because he was already in the Army for two years.

So when he left, I virtually took over where he was. So he went to England and I did my one and a half to two years with the Army.

This is permanent Army, isn't it?

You could join it—it was the permanent Army, I suppose you mean, but I wasn't in permanently.

No, and you joined as a medical officer?

I joined as a medical officer.

Where were you based?

Yeronga Camp Base Hospital in Yeronga Brisbane.

Is that when you started playing rugby?

With the Army, yes.

How many—were you a fairly strong team?

We were actually a strong team, because at that time the Army somehow was introduced into the A Grade rugby system in Brisbane. I don't know the background to that, but it was the time of the national service traineeship and there were a lot of young good footballers in that.

One of my jobs was to examine all these young guys that had come in for their short term with the national service trainees so that's how I think—that was a great help for the rugby, because we had a fairly strong side, and did quite well. I haven't got any details of the games, but we were quite a strong side.

For how long did you play for the Army Rugby Union?

Two years, two seasons.

During that time, was that when you were picked for the Wallabies?

That is correct, and that's when I was picked. I was picked for the Wallabies in 1956 for a game down in Sydney against New Zealand, and the team then was selected to tour the UK, and I was left out, and that caused a bit of a decry up in Queensland here.

But in 1958 Australia toured New Zealand and I was captain for that, and I was still in the Army then, when I was captain of the Australian touring side to New Zealand.

With the Wallabies?

Yes.

So presumably you got time off for that from the Army?

Yes.

How long did you play with your university team?

From 1951 to 1958, so about seven years. And in 1956 I was selected to play for Australia in Australia, one game, against New Zealand. We got beaten. I was dropped for the tour—the next year was to the UK and I wasn't invited. A lot of criticism. It was better for me that I didn't go because the next year I captained Australia, in 1958, whilst in the Army, and a tour of New Zealand. We did very well on that tour.

You were pleased about that?

Well I was, yes, in retrospect. I wasn't at the time, being dropped, but then I didn't think properly—I came out of it very well, put it that way.

Do you remember 'Danny' Kaye?

I remember him, and he played in the backs and he was a very good player, but I haven't seen him since.

Was he Army as well?

I think he was Army. I, in the back of my mind, thought he was from Victoria. Whereas van Gelder, the other Army player, I think was from South Australia.

Did they go on and do more significant contribution to the Army rugby do you know?

I think so. They were good players, you know, they weren't in the first side, but they filled adequately for the other games, so no, they were very good.

So they weren't in the Wallabies with you when you were seconded to the Wallabies to play in New Zealand.

Yes.

Were they involved in the team that you captained in New Zealand, the Wallabies?

Yes, the three main games.

What were the highlights then of the tour of New Zealand?

Well, you know, New Zealand was considered to be the best Rugby Union side in the world. There was always opposition between Australia and New Zealand. It's a thing that's been there and still is and always will be, you know. New Zealand are fanatical about their rugby and they had a marvellous tour of the UK later on—they were always a good side and it's always a great honour to go to New Zealand and play them you know.

Any low lights, any problems or difficulties?

There were no problems at all, no. It was a marvellous tour. You know, it's laid on in New Zealand, as you know, any team that tours New Zealand wherever you go, you're welcomed and it's a religion to them, and it was then, and is now.

Then when you returned, you were still in the Army, weren't you?

How much longer did you then serve in the Army?

When I came back I went overseas. I must have completed my two years in the Army and then went over to do my studies overseas.

That was your post-graduate studies, wasn't it?

Post-graduate, yes. Those days in medicine people went overseas to get these higher qualifications. I don't know why that was, but it was, and it turns out you get a lot of good experience, you know.

Yes, and that was in surgery, I think you told me?

I initially did general surgery, but then changed to gynaecology over there. See you have to do so many years of a subject before you can sit for the examination. I couldn't do that in Australia—with the rugby in the background, because that helped me overseas, you know, already played rugby, good, he can join us in rugby over there. It was for me, quite easy to get jobs at good hospitals. So what you had to do is go overseas, work for two years in obstetrics and gynaecology before you can sit for any examination. So that's why I was over in England for four or five years.

In retrospect, your Army experience—was that a good experience do you think?

I suppose from the rugby point of view not so much, but it was interesting. I enjoyed it very much and met a lot of nice people. As I said to you before, my brother was involved in the Army before me and he gave me a lot of advice, but yes, I enjoyed it very much.

Then you came back to Australia when?

> I came back to Australia then—wait til I get my little piece of paper—it was about 1964. So I was over there for quite a while.
>
> I only played for a year or so when I came back from England and I played a lot of rugby, as I said, before in England. I played against the All Blacks over there on two occasions, and involved a lot with the Scottish side.
>
> I have Scottish ancestry, you see, and they thought I could play for Scotland, but they stopped that way of getting into the Scottish side, so I didn't play there, but I did play against the All Blacks in England and then we came back and played for the London Scottish and London Counties and then came back in 1964 to Australia when I was coach captain of West Rugby Union.

Thank you, Chilla.

www.ingramcontent.com/pod-product-compliance
Lightning Source LLC
Chambersburg PA
CBHW060945100426

42813CB00016B/2861